KNOWLEDGE
That Leads to Everlasting Life

PUBLISHERS

WATCHTOWER BIBLE AND TRACT SOCIETY OF NEW YORK, INC.
INTERNATIONAL BIBLE STUDENTS ASSOCIATION
BROOKLYN, NEW YORK, U.S.A.

FIRST PRINTING IN ENGLISH:
6,000,000 COPIES

UNLESS OTHERWISE INDICATED,
SCRIPTURE QUOTATIONS ARE FROM THE MODERN-LANGUAGE
NEW WORLD TRANSLATION OF THE HOLY SCRIPTURES—WITH REFERENCES,
1984 EDITION

PHOTO CREDITS

PAGE 20, BACKGROUND: BIBELMUSEUM, MÜNSTER

PAGE 100, STARVATION: MARK PETERS/SIPA PRESS;
SOLDIER: BILL GENTILE/SIPA PRESS; WARPLANES: USAF PHOTO

PAGE 101, POLLUTION: WHO PHOTO BY P. ALMASY;
STREET PEOPLE: ALEXANDRE TOKITAKA/SIPA PRESS

KNOWLEDGE THAT LEADS TO EVERLASTING LIFE   ENGLISH (*kl*-E)
MADE IN THE UNITED STATES OF AMERICA

CONTENTS

Beautiful surroundings like these can be yours forever!

•

What must you do to enjoy them? The answer lies in a special kind of knowledge.

•

This book will help you gain the knowledge that leads to everlasting life.

CHAPTER 1

YOU CAN HAVE A HAPPY FUTURE!

A WARM embrace from someone you love. Hearty laughter during a good meal with dear friends. The pleasure of watching your children cheerfully at play. Moments like these are bright spots in life. For many, however, life seems to present one serious problem after another. If that has been your experience, take heart.

2 It is God's will that you enjoy lasting happiness under the best conditions in wonderful surroundings. This is no mere dream, for God actually offers you the key to such a happy future. That key is knowledge.

3 We are talking about a special kind of knowledge that is far greater than human wisdom. It is "the very knowledge of God." (Proverbs 2:5) Nearly 2,000 years ago, a Bible writer said: "Every house is constructed by someone, but he that constructed all things is God." (Hebrews 3:4) Think of the knowledge that the Maker of all things must possess! The Bible says that God counts and names all the stars. What a staggering thought, since there are hundreds of billions of stars in our own galaxy, and astronomers say that there are about a hundred billion other galaxies! (Psalm 147:4) God also knows all about *us,* so who else could provide better answers to life's important questions?—Matthew 10:30.

1, 2. What does your Creator want for you?
3. What knowledge is the key to happiness, and why can we be sure that God can provide that knowledge?

⁴ Picture two men trying to repair their cars. Frustrated, one man throws down his tools. The other calmly corrects the problem, turns the ignition key, and smiles as the engine starts up and runs smoothly. You would not have a hard time guessing which of the two men had an instruction manual from the manufacturer. Does it not make sense that God would provide instructions to guide us in life? As you may know, the Bible claims to be just that—a book of instruction and guidance from our Creator, designed to impart the knowledge of God.—2 Timothy 3:16.

⁵ If the Bible's claim is true, think of what treasures of knowledge that book must contain! At Proverbs 2:1-5, it urges us to seek wisdom, to dig for it as we would for a hidden treasure—not in the soil of human thinking, but in God's own Word. If we search there, we will "find the very knowledge of God." Since God understands our limitations and needs, he gives us instruction that will help us to lead peaceful, happy lives. (Psalm 103:14; Isaiah 48:17) Furthermore, the knowledge of God offers us exciting good news.

EVERLASTING LIFE!

⁶ The well-known historical figure Jesus Christ described this feature of the knowledge of God in clear terms. He said: "This means *everlasting life,* their taking in knowledge of you, the only true God, and of the one whom you sent forth, Jesus Christ." (John 17:3) Imagine —knowledge that leads to everlasting life!

⁷ Do not quickly dismiss everlasting life as a mere

4. Why should we expect God to provide instructions to guide us, and what book fills this need?
5. How valuable is the knowledge that the Bible contains?
6. What assurance did Jesus Christ give regarding the knowledge of God?
7. What evidence is there that God did not intend for us to die?

dream. Instead, look at the way the human body is made. It is splendidly designed to taste, hear, smell, see, and feel. There is so much on the earth that delights our senses—delicious food, pleasant birdsong, fragrant flowers, beautiful scenery, delightful companionship! And our amazing brain is far more than a supercomputer, for it enables us to appreciate and enjoy all such things. Do you think that our Creator wants us to die and lose all of this? Would it not be more reasonable to conclude that he wants us to live happily and to enjoy life forever? Well, that is what the knowledge of God can mean for you.

LIFE IN PARADISE

⁸ What the Bible says about the future of the earth and mankind might be summed up in one word—Paradise! Jesus Christ spoke of it when he told a dying man: "You will be with me in Paradise." (Luke 23:43) The mention of Paradise no doubt brought to that man's mind the happy state of our first parents, Adam and Eve. When God created them, they were perfect and lived in a gardenlike park that the Creator had designed and planted. It was fittingly called the garden of Eden, which name denotes pleasure.

⁹ How delightful that garden was! It was a real paradise. Among its beautiful trees were those bearing delicious fruit. As Adam and Eve explored their domain, drank from its sweet waters, and gathered fruit from its trees, they had no reason to be anxious or fearful. Even animals posed no threat, for God had placed the man and his wife in loving dominion over all of them. In addition, the first human pair had vibrant health. As long as they remained obedient to God, an eternal, happy future lay before them. They were given the satisfying work of caring for their wonderful Paradise home. Further, God

8. What does the Bible say about the future of mankind?
9. What was it like to live in the original Paradise?

gave Adam and Eve the mandate to "fill the earth and subdue it." They and their offspring were to extend the borders of Paradise until our entire planet became a place of beauty and delight.—Genesis 1:28.

¹⁰ When Jesus mentioned Paradise, however, he was not asking a dying man to think about the distant past. No, Jesus was speaking about the future! He knew that our entire earthly home would become a paradise. God would thus fulfill his original purpose for mankind and our earth. (Isaiah 55:10, 11) Yes, Paradise will be restored! And what will it be like? Let God's Word, the Holy Bible, answer.

LIFE IN THE RESTORED PARADISE

¹¹ *Sickness, old age, and death will no longer exist.* "At that time the eyes of the blind ones will be opened, and the very ears of the deaf ones will be unstopped. At that time the lame one will climb up just as a stag does, and the tongue of the speechless one will cry out in gladness." (Isaiah 35:5, 6) "God himself will be with [mankind]. And he will wipe out every tear from their eyes, and death will be no more, neither will mourning nor outcry nor pain be anymore. The former things have passed away."—Revelation 21:3, 4.

¹² *Crime, violence, and wickedness will be gone forever.* "Evildoers themselves will be cut off . . . Just a little while longer, and the wicked one will be no more . . . He will not be. But the meek ones themselves will possess the earth." (Psalm 37:9-11) "As regards the wicked, they will be cut off from the very earth; and as for the treacherous, they will be torn away from it."—Proverbs 2:22.

---

10. When Jesus spoke of Paradise, what did he have in mind?
11. In the restored Paradise, what will happen to sickness, old age, and death?
12. Why can we be sure that there will be no crime, violence, and wickedness in the future Paradise?

[13] *Peace will prevail earth wide.* "He [God] is making wars to cease to the extremity of the earth. The bow he breaks apart and does cut the spear in pieces." (Psalm 46:9) "The righteous one will sprout, and the abundance of peace until the moon is no more."—Psalm 72:7.

[14] *Housing will be secure and work satisfying.* "They will certainly build houses and have occupancy . . . They will not build and someone else have occupancy; they will not plant and someone else do the eating. For like the days of a tree will the days of my people be; and the work of their own hands my chosen ones will use to the full. They will not toil for nothing, nor will they bring to birth for disturbance."—Isaiah 65:21-23.

[15] *Healthful food will be available in abundance.* "There will come to be plenty of grain on the earth; on the top of the mountains there will be an overflow." (Psalm 72:16) "The earth itself will certainly give its produce; God, our God, will bless us."—Psalm 67:6.

[16] *Everlasting life on a paradise earth will be delightful.* "The righteous themselves will possess the earth, and they will reside forever upon it." (Psalm 37:29) "The wilderness and the waterless region will exult, and the desert plain will be joyful and blossom as the saffron."—Isaiah 35:1.

KNOWLEDGE AND YOUR FUTURE

[17] If life in Paradise appeals to you, let nothing hold you back from gaining the knowledge of God. He loves mankind and will bring about the changes needed to make the

---

13. How will God bring about peace?
14, 15. What does the Bible say about housing, work, and food in the restored Paradise?
16. Why will life in Paradise be delightful?
17. (a) What should you do if life in Paradise appeals to you? (b) How do we know that God will bring about great changes on the earth?

earth a paradise. After all, if you had the power to end the misery and injustice so prevalent in the world, would you not do so? Would we expect God to do less? Actually, the Bible speaks in vivid terms of a time when God will remove this strife-ridden system and replace it with a perfect, righteous rule. (Daniel 2:44) But the Bible does much more than tell us about all of this. It shows us how we can survive into God's promised new world.—2 Peter 3:13; 1 John 2:17.

[18] The knowledge of God can also do much for you right now. Life's deepest and most disturbing questions are answered in the Bible. Accepting its guidance will help you to develop a friendship with God. What a grand privilege! And this will enable you to enjoy the peace that God alone can give. (Romans 15:13, 33) As you begin to take in this vital knowledge, you are embarking on the most important and rewarding endeavor of your life. You will never regret acquiring the knowledge of God that leads to everlasting life.

[19] We have referred to the Bible as the book containing the knowledge of God. Yet, how do we know that it is, not a book of human wisdom, but something far greater? We will consider this question in the next chapter.

---

18. What can the knowledge of God do for you now?
19. What question will we consider in the next chapter?

TEST YOUR KNOWLEDGE

Why can the knowledge of God lead you
to eternal happiness?

•

What will life be like in the coming
earthly Paradise?

•

Why will you benefit from taking in the
knowledge of God now?

CHAPTER 2

THE BOOK THAT REVEALS THE KNOWLEDGE OF GOD

IT IS only reasonable that our loving Creator would provide a book of instruction and guidance for mankind. And do you not agree that humans need guidance?

2 More than 2,500 years ago, a prophet and historian wrote: "It does not belong to man who is walking even to direct his step." (Jeremiah 10:23) Today, the truthfulness of that statement is more evident than ever. Thus, historian William H. McNeill notes: "The human adventure on the face of this planet has been an almost uninterrupted series of crises and disruptions of society's established order."

3 The Bible fills all our needs for wise direction. True, many are overwhelmed when they first look through the Bible. It is a big book, and some portions of it are not easy to understand. But if you were given a legal document outlining what you had to do in order to receive a valuable inheritance, would you not take the time to study it carefully? If you found certain parts of the document hard to understand, likely you would get the help of someone experienced in such matters. Why not approach

---

1, 2. Why do we need our Creator's guidance?
3, 4. (a) How should we approach a study of the Bible? (b) How will we proceed with an examination of the Bible?

the Bible with a similar attitude? (Acts 17:11) More is at stake than a material inheritance. As we learned in the previous chapter, the knowledge of God can lead to everlasting life.

⁴ Let us examine the book that reveals the knowledge of God. We will first give a brief overview of the Bible. Then we will discuss reasons why many informed people believe that it is the inspired Word of God.

WHAT THE BIBLE CONTAINS

⁵ The Bible contains 66 books in two sections, often called the Old Testament and the New Testament. Thirty-nine Bible books were written mainly in Hebrew and 27 in Greek. The Hebrew Scriptures, consisting of Genesis through Malachi, cover creation as well as the first 3,500 years of human history. Examining this part of the Bible, we learn about God's dealings with the Israelites—from their birth as a nation in the 16th century B.C.E. on into the 5th century B.C.E.* The Greek Scriptures, containing the books of Matthew through Revelation, focus on the teachings and activities of Jesus Christ and his disciples during the first century C.E.

⁶ Some claim that the "Old Testament" is for Jews and the "New Testament" is for Christians. But according to 2 Timothy 3:16, "*all* Scripture is inspired of God and beneficial." Therefore, a proper study of the Scriptures must include the entire Bible. Actually, the two parts of the Bible complement each other, blending harmoniously to develop an overall theme.

---

* B.C.E. means "before the Common Era," which is more accurate than B.C. ("before Christ"). C.E. denotes "Common Era," often called A.D., for *anno Domini,* meaning "in the year of our Lord."

---

5. (a) What is contained in the Hebrew Scriptures? (b) What do the Greek Scriptures contain?
6. Why should we study the entire Bible?

PUT YOUR BIBLE TO GOOD USE

Becoming familiar with the Bible need not be difficult. Use its table of contents to learn the order and location of Bible books.

The books of the Bible have chapters and verses for easy reference. The chapter divisions were added during the 13th century, and a 16th-century French printer apparently divided the Greek Scriptures into the present-day verses. The first complete Bible to have both chapter and verse numbers was a French edition, published in 1553.

When scriptures are cited in this book, the first number indicates the chapter, and the next denotes the verse. For example, the citation "Proverbs 2:5" means the book of Proverbs, chapter 2, verse 5. By looking up the cited scriptures, you will soon feel at ease locating Bible texts.

The best way to become familiar with the Bible is to read it daily. At first, this may seem challenging. But if you read from three to five chapters a day, depending on their length, you will complete the reading of the entire Bible in a year. Why not start today?

[7] Perhaps you have attended religious services for years and have heard some of the Bible read aloud. Or you may have read excerpts from it yourself. Did you know that the Bible has a common thread from Genesis through Revelation? Yes, a harmonious theme permeates the Bible. What is that theme? It is the vindication of God's right to rule mankind and the realization of his loving purpose by means of his Kingdom. Later, we will see just how God will fulfill this purpose.

[8] In addition to outlining God's purpose, the Bible reveals his personality. For example, from the Bible we learn that God has feelings and that the choices we make matter to him. (Psalm 78:40, 41; Proverbs 27:11; Ezekiel 33:11) Psalm 103:8-14 says that God is "merciful and gracious, slow to anger and abundant in loving-kindness."

---

7. What is the theme of the Bible?
8. What does the Bible reveal about God's personality?

He treats us compassionately, 'remembering that we are made of mere dust' and return to it at death. (Genesis 2:7; 3:19) What marvelous qualities he displays! Is this not the kind of God you want to worship?

⁹ The Bible gives us a clear view of God's standards. These are sometimes stated as laws. More often, however, they are reflected in principles taught by means of object lessons. God had certain events in ancient Israelite history written down for our benefit. These candid accounts show what happens when people work in harmony with God's purpose, as well as the sad outcome when they go their own way. (1 Kings 5:4; 11:4-6; 2 Chronicles 15:8-15) Reading such real-life accounts will undoubtedly touch our hearts. If we try to visualize the events recorded, we can identify with the people involved in them. Thus, we can benefit from good examples and can avoid the pitfalls that ensnared wrongdoers. However, this vital question requires an answer: How can we be sure that what we read in the Bible is actually inspired of God?

CAN YOU TRUST THE BIBLE?

¹⁰ Perhaps you have noticed that many books offering advice become outdated in just a few years. What about the Bible? It is very old, and almost 2,000 years have passed since its last words were penned. Some therefore feel that it is not applicable to our modern age. But if the Bible is inspired of God, its advice should always be up-to-date despite its great age. The Scriptures should still be "beneficial for teaching, for reproving, for setting things straight, for disciplining in righteousness, that the man of God may be fully competent, completely equipped for every good work."—2 Timothy 3:16, 17.

---

9. How does the Bible give us a clear view of God's standards, and how can we benefit from such knowledge?

10. (a) Why do some feel that the Bible is out-of-date? (b) What does 2 Timothy 3:16, 17 tell us about the Bible?

[11] Close examination reveals that Bible principles apply just as much today as they did when they were first put down in writing. When it comes to human nature, for instance, the Bible reflects keen understanding that applies to every generation of mankind. We can easily see this in Jesus' Sermon on the Mount, found in the book of Matthew, chapters 5 to 7. This sermon so impressed the late Indian leader Mohandas K. Gandhi that he reportedly told a British official: "When your country and mine shall get together on the teachings laid down by Christ in this Sermon on the Mount, we shall have solved the problems not only of our countries but those of the whole world."

[12] No wonder people are impressed by Jesus' teachings! In the Sermon on the Mount, he showed us the way to true happiness. He explained how to settle disputes. Jesus provided instruction on how to pray. He pointed out the wisest attitude to have toward material needs and gave the Golden Rule for proper relationships with others. How to detect religious frauds and how to have a secure future were also among the points covered in this sermon.

[13] In the Sermon on the Mount and throughout the rest of its pages, the Bible clearly tells us what to do and what to avoid in order to improve our lot in life. So practical is its counsel that one educator was moved to say: "Although being a high-school counselor with bachelor's and master's degrees and having read a large number of books on mental health and psychology, I discovered that the Bible's counsel on such things as having a successful marriage, preventing juvenile delinquency and how to gain and keep friends is far superior to anything I had read or studied in college." In addition to being practical and up-to-date, the Bible is dependable.

11-13. Why can we say that the Bible is practical for our day?

ACCURATE AND RELIABLE

[14] Though the Bible is not a science textbook, it is scientifically accurate. For example, at a time when most people believed that the earth was flat, the prophet Isaiah referred to it as a "circle" (Hebrew, *chugh,* which here carries the idea of "sphere"). (Isaiah 40:22) The idea of a spherical earth was not widely accepted until thousands of years after Isaiah's day. Furthermore, Job 26:7—written more than 3,000 years ago—states that God is "hanging the earth upon nothing." Says one Bible scholar: "How Job knew the truth, demonstrated by astronomy, that the earth hangs self-poised in empty space, is a question not easily solved by those who deny the inspiration of Holy Scripture."

[15] The style of reporting found in the Bible also strengthens our confidence in this age-old book. Unlike myths, the events covered in the Bible are linked to specific people and dates. (1 Kings 14:25; Isaiah 36:1; Luke 3: 1, 2) And whereas ancient historians nearly always exaggerated the victories of their rulers and hid their defeats and mistakes, the Bible writers were candid and honest —even about their own serious sins.—Numbers 20:7-13; 2 Samuel 12:7-14; 24:10.

A BOOK OF PROPHECY

[16] Fulfilled prophecy gives conclusive evidence that the Bible is inspired of God. The Bible contains many prophecies that have been fulfilled in detail. Obviously, mere humans could not be responsible for this. What, then, is behind these prophecies? The Bible itself says that "prophecy was at no time brought by man's will, but men

14. What shows that the Bible is scientifically accurate?
15. How is confidence in the Bible strengthened by its style of reporting?
16. What is the strongest evidence that the Bible is inspired of God?

spoke from God as they were borne along by holy spirit," or God's active force. (2 Peter 1:21) Consider some examples.

¹⁷ *The fall of Babylon.* Isaiah and Jeremiah both foretold Babylon's fall to the Medes and the Persians. Remarkably, Isaiah's prophecy about this event was recorded some 200 years before Babylon was conquered! The following aspects of prophecy are now matters of historical record: the drying up of the Euphrates River by diverting its waters to an artificial lake (Isaiah 44:27; Jeremiah 50:38); a careless lack of security at Babylon's river gates (Isaiah 45:1); and the conquest by a ruler named Cyrus. —Isaiah 44:28.

¹⁸ *The rise and fall of "the king of Greece."* In a vision, Daniel saw a male goat strike down a ram, breaking its two horns. Then, the goat's great horn was broken, and four horns came up in its place. (Daniel 8:1-8) To Daniel it was explained: "The ram that you saw possessing the two horns stands for the kings of Media and Persia. And the hairy he-goat stands for the king of Greece; and as for the great horn that was between its eyes, it stands for the first king. And that one having been broken, so that there were four that finally stood up instead of it, there are four kingdoms from his nation that will stand up, but not with his power." (Daniel 8:20-22) True to this prophecy, some two centuries later, "the king of Greece," Alexander the Great, overthrew the two-horned Medo-Persian Empire. Alexander died in 323 B.C.E. and was eventually replaced by four of his generals. However, none of these subsequent kingdoms matched the power of Alexander's empire.

---

17. What prophecies foretold the fall of Babylon, and how were these fulfilled?
18. How was Bible prophecy fulfilled in the rise and fall of "the king of Greece"?

THE BIBLE—A UNIQUE BOOK

• The Bible is "inspired of God." (2 Timothy 3:16) Although humans penned the words, God directed their thoughts, so that the Bible is really "the word of God." —1 Thessalonians 2:13.

• The Bible was written over a period of 16 centuries, by some 40 contributors from diverse backgrounds. Nevertheless, the finished product is harmonious from beginning to end.

• The Bible has survived more controversy than any other book. During the Middle Ages, people were burned at the stake simply for possessing a copy of the Scriptures.

• The Bible is the number one best-seller in the world. It has been translated, in whole or in part, into over 2,000 languages. Billions of copies have been printed, and there is hardly a place on earth where a copy cannot be found.

• The oldest portion of the Bible dates back to the 16th century B.C.E. This is before the appearance of the Hindu *Rig-Veda* (in about 1300 B.C.E.), or the Buddhist "Canon of the Three Baskets" (fifth century B.C.E.), or the Islamic Koran (seventh century C.E.), as well as the Shinto *Nihongi* (720 C.E.).

---

¹⁹ *The life of Jesus Christ.* The Hebrew Scriptures contain scores of prophecies fulfilled in the birth, ministry, death, and resurrection of Jesus. For example, more than 700 years in advance, Micah foretold that the Messiah, or Christ, would be born in Bethlehem. (Micah 5:2; Luke 2: 4-7) Micah's contemporary Isaiah foretold that the Messiah would be struck and spit upon. (Isaiah 50:6; Matthew 26:67) Five hundred years in advance, Zechariah prophesied that the Messiah would be betrayed for 30 pieces of silver. (Zechariah 11:12; Matthew 26:15) More than a thousand years beforehand, David foretold circumstances associated with the death of Jesus the Messiah. (Psalm 22:7, 8, 18; Matthew 27:35, 39-43) And some five centuries in advance, Daniel's prophecy revealed when the Messiah would appear as well as the length of his ministry

---

19. What prophecies were fulfilled in Jesus Christ?

and the time of his death. (Daniel 9:24-27) This is just a sampling of the prophecies fulfilled in Jesus Christ. You will find it rewarding to read much more about him later.

[20] Many other long-range Bible prophecies have already been fulfilled. 'But,' you may ask, 'how does this affect my life?' Well, if someone told you the truth for many years, would you suddenly doubt him when he said something new? No! God has told the truth throughout the Bible. Should this not build your trust in what the Bible promises, such as its prophecies regarding a coming earthly paradise? Indeed, we can have the same confidence as did Paul, one of Jesus' first-century disciples, who wrote that 'God cannot lie.' (Titus 1:2) Furthermore, when we read the Scriptures and apply their counsel, we are exercising wisdom that humans cannot achieve on their own, for the Bible is the book that reveals the knowledge of God that leads to everlasting life.

"FORM A LONGING" FOR THE KNOWLEDGE OF GOD

[21] As you study the Bible, you are likely to learn things that differ from what you have been taught in the past. You may even find that some of your cherished religious customs do not please God. You will learn that God has standards of right and wrong higher than those common in this permissive world. This may seem overwhelming at first. But be patient! Carefully examine the Scriptures to find the knowledge of God. Be open to the possibility that the Bible's counsel may call for an adjustment in your thinking and actions.

[22] Well-meaning friends and relatives may oppose your

---

20. The Bible's perfect record of fulfilled prophecy should give us what confidence?
21. What should you do if some things you learn from the Bible seem overwhelming?
22. Why are you studying the Bible, and how can you help others understand this?

study of the Bible, but Jesus said: "Everyone, then, that confesses union with me before men, I will also confess union with him before my Father who is in the heavens; but whoever disowns me before men, I will also disown him before my Father who is in the heavens." (Matthew 10:32, 33) Some may fear that you will become involved with a cult or will turn into a fanatic. In reality, however, you are merely striving to gain accurate knowledge of God and of his truth. (1 Timothy 2:3, 4) To help others understand this, be reasonable, not argumentative, when you speak to them about what you are learning. (Philippians 4:5) Remember that many are "won without a word" when they see evidence that Bible knowledge really benefits people.—1 Peter 3:1, 2.

²³ The Bible urges us: "As newborn infants, form a longing for the unadulterated milk belonging to the word." (1 Peter 2:2) An infant depends on nourishment from its mother and is insistent on having that need met. Similarly, we are dependent on knowledge from God. "Form a longing" for his Word by continuing your study. Indeed, make it your goal to read the Bible daily. (Psalm 1:1-3) This will bring you rich blessings, for Psalm 19:11 says of God's laws: "In the keeping of them there is a large reward."

23. How can you "form a longing" for the knowledge of God?

TEST YOUR KNOWLEDGE

In what ways is the Bible
like no other book?

•

Why can you trust the Bible?

•

What proves to you that the Bible
is God's inspired Word?

WHO IS THE TRUE GOD?

WHEN you look at the sky on a clear night, are you not amazed to see so many stars? How do you account for their existence? And what about the living things on earth—colorful flowers, birds with their delightful songs, powerful whales that leap in the ocean? The list goes on and on. All of this could not have come about by chance. No wonder many agree with the Bible's opening words: "In the beginning God created the heavens and the earth"!—Genesis 1:1.

² Mankind is greatly divided on the question of God. Some think that God is an impersonal force. Millions worship dead ancestors, believing that God is too remote to be approached. But the Bible reveals that the true God is a real person who shows warm interest in us as individuals. That is why it encourages us to "seek God," saying: "He is not far off from each one of us."—Acts 17:27.

³ What does God look like? A few of his servants have seen visions of his glorious presence. In these he has symbolized himself as seated on a throne, awesome brightness extending from him. However, those who beheld such visions never described a distinct face. (Daniel 7: 9, 10; Revelation 4:2, 3) That is because "God is a Spirit";

---

1. Why do many agree with the Bible's opening words?
2. What does the Bible say about God, and what does it encourage us to do?
3. Why is it impossible to make an image of God?

he does not have a physical body. (John 4:24) In fact, it is impossible to make an accurate physical image of our Creator, for "no man has seen God at any time." (John 1:18; Exodus 33:20) Yet, the Bible teaches us much about God.

THE TRUE GOD HAS A NAME

⁴ In the Bible, the true God is identified by such expressions as "God Almighty," "the Most High," "Grand Creator," "Grand Instructor," "Sovereign Lord," and "King of eternity." (Genesis 17:1; Psalm 50:14; Ecclesiastes 12:1; Isaiah 30:20; Acts 4:24; 1 Timothy 1:17) Meditating upon such titles can help us grow in the knowledge of God.

⁵ However, God has a unique name that appears almost 7,000 times in the Hebrew Scriptures alone—more often than any of his titles. Some 1,900 years ago, the Jews superstitiously ceased to pronounce the divine name. Biblical Hebrew was written without vowels. Hence, there is no way to be precise about how Moses, David, or others of ancient times pronounced the four consonants (יהוה) that make up the divine name. Some scholars suggest that God's name may have been pronounced "Yahweh," but they cannot be sure. The English pronunciation "Jehovah" has been in use for centuries, and its equivalent in many languages is widely accepted today.—See Exodus 6:3 and Isaiah 26:4 in the *King James Version*.

WHY YOU SHOULD USE GOD'S NAME

⁶ God's unique name, Jehovah, serves to differentiate him from all other gods. That is why that name appears

---

4. What are some meaningful titles applied to God in the Bible?
5. What is God's name, and how often does it appear in the Hebrew Scriptures?
6. Psalm 83:18 says what about Jehovah, and why should we use his name?

so often in the Bible, especially in its Hebrew text. Many translators fail to use the divine name, but Psalm 83:18 clearly says: "You, whose name is Jehovah, you alone are the Most High over all the earth." So it is appropriate for us to use God's personal name when we speak of him.

⁷ The name Jehovah is a form of a Hebrew verb meaning "to become." Thus, God's name means "He Causes to Become." Jehovah God thereby identifies himself as the Great Purposer. He always causes his purposes to become reality. Only the true God can rightly bear this name, for humans can never be sure that their plans will succeed. (James 4:13, 14) Jehovah alone can say: "So my word that goes forth from my mouth will prove to be.... It will have certain success in that for which I have sent it."—Isaiah 55:11.

⁸ The Hebrew patriarchs Abraham, Isaac, and Jacob each "called on the name of Jehovah," but they did not know the full significance of the divine name. (Genesis 21:33; 26:25; 32:9; Exodus 6:3) When Jehovah later revealed his purpose to deliver their descendants, the Israelites, from slavery in Egypt and give them "a land flowing with milk and honey," this may have seemed impossible. (Exodus 3:17) Nevertheless, God emphasized the everlasting significance of his name by telling his prophet Moses: "This is what you are to say to the sons of Israel, 'Jehovah the God of your forefathers, the God of Abraham, the God of Isaac and the God of Jacob, has sent me to you.' This is my name to time indefinite, and this is the memorial of me to generation after generation."—Exodus 3:15.

⁹ Moses asked Pharaoh, the king of Egypt, to let the

---

7. What does the meaning of the name Jehovah teach us about God?
8. What purpose did Jehovah announce through Moses?
9. How did Pharaoh view Jehovah?

Israelites go to worship Jehovah in the wilderness. But Pharaoh, who himself was viewed as a god and who worshiped other Egyptian gods, replied: "Who is Jehovah, so that I should obey his voice to send Israel away? I do not know Jehovah at all and, what is more, I am not going to send Israel away."—Exodus 5:1, 2.

[10] Jehovah then took progressive action to fulfill his purpose, acting in harmony with the meaning of his name. He brought ten plagues upon the ancient Egyptians. The last plague killed all of Egypt's firstborn, including proud Pharaoh's son. Then the Egyptians were eager for Israel to go. However, some Egyptians were so impressed by Jehovah's power that they joined the Israelites in leaving Egypt.—Exodus 12:35-38.

[11] Stubborn Pharaoh and his army, with hundreds of war chariots, set out to recapture his slaves. As the Egyptians drew near, God miraculously divided the Red Sea so that the Israelites could cross on dry land. When the pursuers entered the seabed, Jehovah "kept taking wheels off their chariots so that they were driving them with difficulty." The Egyptian warriors cried: "Let us flee from any contact with Israel, because Jehovah certainly fights for them against the Egyptians." But it was too late. The vast walls of water crashed down and "covered the war chariots and the cavalrymen belonging to all of Pharaoh's military forces." (Exodus 14:22-25, 28) Jehovah thus made a great name for himself, and that event has not been forgotten to this day.—Joshua 2:9-11.

[12] The name that God has made for himself has great

---

10. In ancient Egypt, what action did Jehovah take to fulfill his purpose involving the Israelites?
11. What miracle did Jehovah perform at the Red Sea, and what were his enemies forced to acknowledge?
12, 13. (a) God's name has what meaning for us today? (b) What do people urgently need to learn, and why?

meaning for us today. His name, Jehovah, stands as a guarantee that all he has purposed he will cause to come true. That includes accomplishing his original purpose that our earth become a paradise. (Genesis 1:28; 2:8) To that end, God will eliminate all opposers of his sovereignty today, for he has stated: "They will have to know that I am Jehovah." (Ezekiel 38:23) Then God will fulfill his promise to deliver his worshipers into a new world of righteousness.—2 Peter 3:13.

¹³ All who want God's favor must learn to call upon his name in faith. The Bible promises: "Everyone who calls on the name of Jehovah will be saved." (Romans 10:13) Yes, the name Jehovah has rich meaning. Calling upon Jehovah as your God and Deliverer can lead you to endless happiness.

QUALITIES OF THE TRUE GOD

¹⁴ A study of Israel's deliverance from Egypt highlights four basic qualities that God possesses in perfect balance. His dealings with Pharaoh revealed his awesome *power*. (Exodus 9:16) The masterful way God handled that complex situation showed his matchless *wisdom*. (Romans 11:33) He revealed his *justice* in meting out punishment to stubborn opposers and oppressors of his people. (Deuteronomy 32:4) A preeminent quality of God is *love*. Jehovah showed outstanding love by fulfilling his promise respecting Abraham's descendants. (Deuteronomy 7:8) He also showed love by allowing some Egyptians to forsake false gods and benefit greatly by taking their stand for the only true God.

¹⁵ As you read the Bible, you will notice that love is God's principal attribute, and he demonstrates it in many ways. For instance, it was out of love that he

14. What basic qualities of God does the Bible highlight?
15, 16. In what ways has God shown love?

became a Creator and first shared the joy of life with spirit creatures. Those hundreds of millions of angels love God and praise him. (Job 38:4, 7; Daniel 7:10) God also showed love in creating the earth and preparing it for happy human existence.—Genesis 1:1, 26-28; Psalm 115:16.

16 We benefit from God's love in ways too numerous to mention. For one thing, God has lovingly made our bodies in such a marvelous way that we can enjoy life. (Psalm 139:14) His love is shown in that he provides "rains from heaven and fruitful seasons, filling [our] hearts to the full with food and good cheer." (Acts 14:17) God even "makes his sun rise upon wicked people and good and makes it rain upon righteous people and unrighteous." (Matthew 5:45) Love also moves our Creator to help us gain the knowledge of God and serve him happily as his worshipers. Indeed, "God is love." (1 John 4:8) But there is much more to his personality.

"A GOD MERCIFUL AND GRACIOUS"

17 After the Israelites crossed the Red Sea, they still needed to know God better. Moses felt this need and prayed: "If, please, I have found favor in your eyes, make me know, please, your ways, that I may know you, in order that I may find favor in your eyes." (Exodus 33:13) Moses got to know God better upon hearing God's own declaration: "Jehovah, Jehovah, a God merciful and gracious, slow to anger and abundant in loving-kindness and truth, preserving loving-kindness for thousands, pardoning error and transgression and sin, but by no means will he give exemption from punishment." (Exodus 34:6, 7) God balances his love with justice, not shielding willful sinners from the consequences of their wrongdoing.

17. What do we learn about God at Exodus 34:6, 7?

How well do you know the Creator of all things?

¹⁸ As Moses learned, Jehovah shows mercy. A merciful person has pity on those who suffer and tries to bring them relief. Thus God has shown compassion for mankind by making provision for permanent relief from suffering, sickness, and death. (Revelation 21:3-5) Worshipers of God may experience calamities because of conditions in this wicked world, or they may act unwisely and meet up with trouble. But if they humbly turn to Jehovah for assistance, he will comfort and help them. Why? Because he mercifully shows tender regard for his worshipers.—Psalm 86:15; 1 Peter 5:6, 7.

¹⁹ Many people in authority treat others harshly. In contrast, how gracious Jehovah is toward his humble servants! Though he is the highest authority in the universe, he shows outstanding kindness in a general way

18. How has Jehovah proved to be merciful?
19. Why can we say that God is gracious?

to all mankind. (Psalm 8:3, 4; Luke 6:35) Jehovah is also gracious to individuals, answering their specific pleas for favor. (Exodus 22:26, 27; Luke 18:13, 14) Of course, God is not obligated to show favor or mercy to anyone. (Exodus 33:19) Therefore, we need to manifest deep appreciation for God's mercy and graciousness.—Psalm 145:1, 8.

SLOW TO ANGER, IMPARTIAL, AND RIGHTEOUS

20 Jehovah is slow to anger. Yet, this does not mean that he does not take action, for he did so in destroying stubborn Pharaoh and his army in the Red Sea. Jehovah is also impartial. Hence, his favored people, the Israelites, eventually lost his favor because of their persistent wrongdoing. God accepts as his worshipers people from all nations, but only those who conform to his righteous ways.—Acts 10:34, 35.

21 The Bible book of Revelation highlights the importance of learning about God's "righteous decrees." It tells us that heavenly creatures sing: "Great and wonderful are your works, Jehovah God, the Almighty. Righteous and true are your ways, King of eternity. Who will not really fear you, Jehovah, and glorify your name, because you alone are loyal? For all the nations will come and worship before you, because your righteous decrees have been made manifest." (Revelation 15:2-4) We show wholesome fear of Jehovah, or reverence for him, by conforming to what he says is right. This is made easier by reminding ourselves of God's wisdom and love. All his commands are for our good.—Isaiah 48:17, 18.

"JEHOVAH OUR GOD IS ONE"

22 The ancient Egyptians worshiped many gods, but Je-

---

20. What shows that Jehovah is both slow to anger and impartial?
21. (a) What does Revelation 15:2-4 teach us about God? (b) What will make it easier for us to do what God says is right?
22. Why do those who accept the Bible not worship a Trinity?

hovah is "a God exacting exclusive devotion." (Exodus 20:5) Moses reminded the Israelites that "Jehovah our God is *one* Jehovah." (Deuteronomy 6:4) Jesus Christ repeated those words. (Mark 12:28, 29) Therefore, those who accept the Bible as God's Word do not worship a Trinity consisting of three persons or gods in one. In fact, the word "Trinity" does not even appear in the Bible. The true God is one Person, separate from Jesus Christ. (John 14:28; 1 Corinthians 15:28) God's holy spirit is not a person. It is Jehovah's active force, used by the Almighty to accomplish his purposes.—Genesis 1:2; Acts 2:1-4, 32, 33; 2 Peter 1:20, 21.

[23] When you consider how wonderful Jehovah is, do you not agree that he deserves your worship? As you study his Word, the Bible, you will get to know him better and will learn what he requires of you for your eternal welfare and happiness. (Matthew 5:3, 6) In addition, your love for God will grow. That is fitting, for Jesus said: "You must love Jehovah your God with your whole heart and with your whole soul and with your whole mind and with your whole strength." (Mark 12:30) Obviously, Jesus had such love for God. But what does the Bible reveal about Jesus Christ? What is his role in Jehovah's purpose?

---

23. (a) How will your love for God grow? (b) What did Jesus say about loving God, and what do we need to learn about Christ?

TEST YOUR KNOWLEDGE

What is God's name, and how often is it used in the Hebrew Scriptures?
•
Why should you use God's name?
•
What qualities of Jehovah God especially appeal to you?

CHAPTER 4

JESUS CHRIST
THE KEY TO THE KNOWLEDGE OF GOD

YOU are standing at the door, fumbling with your keys. It is cold and dark, and you are eager to get inside—but the key does not work. It looks right, yet the lock will not budge. How frustrating! You look at your keys again. Are you using the right one? Has someone damaged the key?

[2] That is a fair picture of what this world's religious confusion has done with the knowledge of God. In effect, many have tampered with the key that opens it up to our understanding—Jesus Christ. Some religions have removed the key, ignoring Jesus altogether. Others have distorted Jesus' role, worshiping him as Almighty God. In any case, the knowledge of God is closed to us without an accurate understanding of this principal figure, Jesus Christ.

[3] You may recall that Jesus said: "This means everlasting life, their taking in knowledge of you, the only true God, and of the one whom you sent forth, Jesus Christ." (John 17:3) In saying this, Jesus was not being boastful.

1, 2. How have the world's religions tampered with the key to the knowledge of God?

3. Why might Jesus be called the key to the knowledge of God?

The Scriptures repeatedly emphasize the need for *accurate* knowledge of Christ. (Ephesians 4:13; Colossians 2:2; 2 Peter 1:8; 2:20) "To [Jesus Christ] all the prophets bear witness," noted the apostle Peter. (Acts 10:43) And the apostle Paul wrote: "Carefully concealed in [Jesus] are all the treasures of wisdom and of knowledge." (Colossians 2:3) Paul even said that all of Jehovah's promises come true because of Jesus. (2 Corinthians 1:20) So Jesus Christ is the very key to the knowledge of God. Our knowledge of Jesus must be free of any distortions as to his nature and as to his role in God's arrangement. But why do Jesus' followers consider him to be central to God's purposes?

THE PROMISED MESSIAH

⁴ From the days of the faithful man Abel, God's servants had eagerly looked forward to the Seed foretold by Jehovah God himself. (Genesis 3:15; 4:1-8; Hebrews 11:4) It had been revealed that the Seed would serve God's purpose as the Messiah, meaning "Anointed One." He would "finish off sin," and the glories of his Kingdom were foretold in the psalms. (Daniel 9:24-26; Psalm 72:1-20) Who would prove to be the Messiah?

⁵ Imagine the excitement felt by a young Jew named Andrew when he listened to the words of Jesus of Nazareth. Andrew rushed to his brother Simon Peter and told him: "We have found the Messiah." (John 1:41) Jesus' disciples were convinced that he was the promised Messiah. (Matthew 16:16) And true Christians have been willing to stake their lives on the belief that Jesus was indeed the foretold Messiah, or Christ. What proof have they had? Let us consider three lines of evidence.

4, 5. What hopes centered on the Messiah, and how did Jesus' disciples view him?

EVIDENCE THAT JESUS WAS THE MESSIAH

⁶ *Jesus' lineage* lays the first basis for identifying him as the promised Messiah. Jehovah had told His servant Abraham that the promised Seed would come from his family. Abraham's son Isaac, Isaac's son Jacob, and Jacob's son Judah each received a similar promise. (Genesis 22:18; 26:2-5; 28:12-15; 49:10) The line of the Messiah's descent was narrowed down centuries later when King David was told that his family line would produce this One. (Psalm 132:11; Isaiah 11:1, 10) The Gospel accounts of Matthew and Luke confirm that Jesus came through that family line. (Matthew 1:1-16; Luke 3:23-38) Though Jesus had many bitter enemies, none of them challenged his well-publicized line of descent. (Matthew 21:9, 15) Clearly, then, his lineage is beyond question. However, the Jews' family records were destroyed when the Romans sacked Jerusalem in 70 C.E. In later times, no one could ever prove a claim to be the promised Messiah.

⁷ *Fulfilled prophecy* is a second line of evidence. Scores of Hebrew Scripture prophecies describe various aspects of the Messiah's life course. In the eighth century B.C.E., the prophet Micah foretold that this great ruler would be born in the insignificant town of Bethlehem. Two towns in Israel were named Bethlehem, but this prophecy specified which one: Bethlehem Ephrathah, where King David had been born. (Micah 5:2) Jesus' parents, Joseph and Mary, lived in Nazareth, some

---

6. (a) What line of descent was to produce the promised Seed, and how do we know that Jesus came through that family line? (b) Why would it be impossible for anyone living after 70 C.E. to prove a claim to be the Messiah?

7. (a) What is a second line of evidence that Jesus was the Messiah? (b) How was Micah 5:2 fulfilled in connection with Jesus?

*God gave Jesus
the power to cure the sick*

90 miles north of Bethlehem. While Mary was pregnant, however, the Roman ruler Caesar Augustus ordered all the people to register in their home cities.* So Joseph had to take his pregnant wife to Bethlehem, where Jesus was born.—Luke 2:1-7.

⁸ In the sixth century B.C.E., the prophet Daniel foretold that "Messiah the Leader" would appear 69 "weeks" after the order went forth to restore and rebuild Jerusalem. (Daniel 9:24, 25) Each one of these "weeks" was seven years long.# According to the Bible and secular history, the order to rebuild Jerusalem was issued in 455 B.C.E. (Nehemiah 2:1-8) So the Messiah was to appear 483 (69 times 7) years after 455 B.C.E. That brings us to 29 C.E., the very year that Jehovah anointed Jesus with holy spirit. Jesus thus became "the Christ" (meaning "Anointed One"), or Messiah.—Luke 3:15, 16, 21, 22.

⁹ Of course, not everyone accepted Jesus as the promised Messiah, and the Scriptures had foretold this. As recorded at Psalm 2:2, King David was divinely inspired to foretell: "The kings of earth take their stand and high officials themselves have massed together as one against

---

* This registration better enabled the Roman Empire to exact taxes. Hence, Augustus unwittingly helped to fulfill a prophecy about a ruler who would 'cause an exactor to pass through the kingdom.' The same prophecy foretold that "the Leader of the covenant," or Messiah, would be "broken" in the days of this ruler's successor. Jesus was killed during the reign of Augustus' successor, Tiberius.—Daniel 11:20-22.

The ancient Jews commonly thought in terms of weeks of years. For instance, just as every seventh day was a Sabbath day, every seventh year was a Sabbath year.—Exodus 20:8-11; 23:10, 11.

---

8. (a) When and with what event did the 69 "weeks" begin? (b) How long were the 69 "weeks," and what happened when they ended?
9. (a) How was Psalm 2:2 fulfilled? (b) What are some other prophecies that were fulfilled in Jesus? (See chart.)

SOME OUTSTANDING MESSIANIC PROPHECIES

PROPHECY	EVENT	FULFILLMENT
HIS EARLY LIFE		
Isaiah 7:14	Born of a virgin	Matthew 1:18-23
Jeremiah 31:15	Babes killed after his birth	Matthew 2:16-18
HIS MINISTRY		
Isaiah 61:1, 2	His commission from God	Luke 4:18-21
Isaiah 9:1, 2	Ministry caused people to see a great light	Matthew 4:13-16
Psalm 69:9	Zealous for Jehovah's house	John 2:13-17
Isaiah 53:1	Not believed in	John 12:37, 38
Zechariah 9:9; Psalm 118:26	Entry into Jerusalem on colt of an ass; hailed as king and as the one coming in Jehovah's name	Matthew 21:1-9
HIS BETRAYAL AND DEATH		
Psalm 41:9; 109:8	One apostle unfaithful; betrays Jesus and is later replaced	Acts 1:15-20
Zechariah 11:12	Betrayed for 30 pieces of silver	Matthew 26:14, 15
Psalm 27:12	False witnesses used against him	Matthew 26:59-61
Psalm 22:18	Lots cast for his garments	John 19:23, 24
Isaiah 53:12	Numbered with sinners	Matthew 27:38
Psalm 22:7, 8	Reviled while dying	Mark 15:29-32
Psalm 69:21	Given vinegar	Mark 15:23, 36
Isaiah 53:5; Zechariah 12:10	Pierced	John 19:34, 37
Isaiah 53:9	Buried with the rich	Matthew 27:57-60
Psalm 16:8-11, ftn.	Raised before corruption	Acts 2:25-32; 13:34-37

Jehovah and against his anointed one." This prophecy suggested that leaders from more than one land would unite in order to attack Jehovah's Anointed One, or Messiah. And so it was. The Jewish religious leaders, King Herod, and the Roman governor Pontius Pilate all played a part in having Jesus put to death. Former enemies Herod and Pilate became fast friends from then on. (Matthew 27:1, 2; Luke 23:10-12; Acts 4:25-28) For further proof that Jesus was the Messiah, please see the accompanying chart entitled "Some Outstanding Messianic Prophecies."

[10] *The testimony of Jehovah God* is a third line of evidence supporting Jesus' Messiahship. Jehovah sent angels to let people know that Jesus was the promised Messiah. (Luke 2:10-14) In fact, during Jesus' earthly life, Jehovah himself spoke from heaven, expressing his approval of Jesus. (Matthew 3:16, 17; 17:1-5) Jehovah God gave Jesus the power to perform miracles. Each one of these was further divine proof that Jesus was the Messiah, for God would never give a fraud power to perform miracles. Jehovah also used his holy spirit to inspire the Gospel accounts, so that the evidence of Jesus' Messiahship became part of the Bible, the most widely translated and distributed book in history.—John 4:25, 26.

[11] In all, these categories of evidence include hundreds of facts that identify Jesus as the promised Messiah. Clearly, then, true Christians have rightly viewed him as 'the one to whom all the prophets bore witness' and the key to the knowledge of God. (Acts 10:43) But there is more to learn about Jesus Christ than the fact that he

---

10. In what ways did Jehovah testify that Jesus was his promised Anointed One?
11. How much evidence is there that Jesus was the Messiah?

was the Messiah. Where did he originate? What was he like?

JESUS' PREHUMAN EXISTENCE

12 Jesus' life course might be divided into three stages. The first began long before he was born on the earth. Micah 5:2 said that the Messiah's origin was "from early times, from the days of time indefinite." And Jesus plainly said that he had come from "the realms above," that is, from heaven. (John 8:23; 16:28) How long had he existed in heaven before coming to the earth?

13 Jesus was called God's "only-begotten Son" because Jehovah created him directly. (John 3:16) As "the firstborn of all creation," Jesus was then used by God to create all other things. (Colossians 1:15; Revelation 3:14) John 1:1 says that "the Word" (Jesus in his prehuman existence) was with God "in the beginning." So the Word was with Jehovah when "the heavens and the earth" were created. God was addressing the Word when He said: "Let us make man in our image." (Genesis 1:1, 26) Likewise, the Word must have been God's beloved "master worker," described at Proverbs 8:22-31 as wisdom personified, laboring at Jehovah's side in the making of all things. After Jehovah brought him into existence, the Word spent ages with God in heaven before becoming a man on earth.

14 No wonder Colossians 1:15 calls Jesus "the image of the invisible God"! Through untold years of close association, the obedient Son came to be just like his Father, Jehovah. This is another reason why Jesus is the key to

---

12, 13. (a) How do we know that Jesus existed in heaven before he came to the earth? (b) Who is "the Word," and what did he do before he became a human?

14. Why is Jesus called "the image of the invisible God"?

the life-giving knowledge of God. Everything Jesus did
while on earth is exactly what Jehovah would have done.
Hence, getting to know Jesus also means increasing our
knowledge of Jehovah. (John 8:28; 14:8-10) Clearly, then,
it is vital to learn more about Jesus Christ.

JESUS' LIFE COURSE ON EARTH

¹⁵ The second stage of Jesus' life course was here
on earth. He willingly submitted as God transferred his
life from heaven to the womb of a faithful Jewish vir-
gin named Mary. Jehovah's powerful holy spirit, or active force, 'overshadowed' Mary, causing her to become
pregnant and eventually give birth to a perfect baby.
(Luke 1:34, 35) Jesus inherited no imperfection, since
his life came from a perfect Source. He was reared in
a humble home as the adopted son of the carpenter Joseph and was the first of several children in the family.
—Isaiah 7:14; Matthew 1:22, 23; Mark 6:3.

¹⁶ Jesus' deep devotion to Jehovah God was already
evident when he was 12 years old. (Luke 2:41-49) After growing up and embarking on his ministry at the
age of 30, Jesus also demonstrated his profound love for
his fellow humans. When God's holy spirit empowered
him to perform miracles, he compassionately healed the
sick, the lame, the maimed, the blind, the deaf, the lep-
rous. (Matthew 8:2-4; 15:30) Jesus fed hungry thousands.
(Matthew 15:35-38) He calmed a storm that threatened
the safety of his friends. (Mark 4:37-39) In fact, he even
resurrected the dead. (John 11:43, 44) These miracles are
well-established facts of history. Even Jesus' enemies ac-

15. How did Jesus come to be born as a perfect baby?

16, 17. (a) Where did Jesus get power to perform miracles, and
what were some of them? (b) What are some qualities that Jesus
displayed?

knowledged that he 'performed many signs.'—John 11: 47, 48.

¹⁷ Jesus traveled throughout his homeland, teaching people about God's Kingdom. (Matthew 4:17) He also set a sterling example of patience and reasonableness. Even when his disciples failed him, he sympathetically remarked: "The spirit, of course, is eager, but the flesh is weak." (Mark 14:37, 38) Yet, Jesus was courageous and forthright with those who despised the truth and oppressed the helpless. (Matthew 23:27-33) Above all, he perfectly imitated his Father's example of love. Jesus was even willing to die so that imperfect mankind would have a hope for the future. No wonder, then, that we may well refer to Jesus as the key to the knowledge of God! Yes, he is the *living* key! But why do we say a *living* key? This brings us to the third stage of his life course.

JESUS TODAY

¹⁸ Though the Bible reports on Jesus' death, he is now alive! In fact, hundreds of people living in the first century C.E. were eyewitnesses of the fact that he had been resurrected. (1 Corinthians 15:3-8) As prophesied, he thereafter sat at his Father's right hand and waited to receive kingly power in heaven. (Psalm 110:1; Hebrews 10: 12, 13) So how should we envision Jesus today? Should we think of him as a helpless baby in a manger? Or as a suffering man being put to death? No. He is a mighty, reigning King! And very soon now, he will manifest his rulership over our troubled earth.

¹⁹ At Revelation 19:11-15, the King Jesus Christ is vividly described as coming with great power to destroy the wicked. How eager this loving heavenly Ruler must be to end the suffering that afflicts millions today! And he is

18. How should we envision Jesus Christ today?
19. What action will Jesus take in the near future?

just as eager to help those striving to imitate the perfect example he set while on earth. (1 Peter 2:21) He wants to preserve them through the rapidly approaching "war of the great day of God the Almighty," often called Armageddon, so that they can live forever as earthly subjects of God's heavenly Kingdom.—Revelation 7:9, 14; 16:14, 16.

[20] During Jesus' foretold Thousand Year Reign of peace, he will perform miracles in behalf of all mankind. (Isaiah 9:6, 7; 11:1-10; Revelation 20:6) Jesus will cure all sickness and will bring an end to death. He will resurrect billions so that they too may have an opportunity to live forever on earth. (John 5:28, 29) You will be thrilled to learn more about his Messianic Kingdom in a later chapter. Be assured of this: We cannot even imagine how wonderful our lives will be under Kingdom rule. How important it is to become better acquainted with Jesus Christ! Yes, it is essential that we never lose sight of Jesus, the living key to the knowledge of God that leads to everlasting life.

20. What will Jesus do for mankind during his Thousand Year Reign?

TEST YOUR KNOWLEDGE

How did Jesus' lineage support his claim to be the Messiah?

•

What are some Messianic prophecies fulfilled in Jesus?

•

How did God directly show that Jesus was his Anointed One?

•

Why is Jesus the living key to the knowledge of God?

CHAPTER 5

WHOSE WORSHIP DOES GOD ACCEPT?

HAVE you ever wondered, 'Whose worship does God accept?' A certain woman may have had such a question come to her mind when she spoke with Jesus Christ near Mount Gerizim in Samaria. Calling attention to a difference between the worship of the Samaritans and that of the Jews, she said: "Our forefathers worshiped in this mountain; but you people say that in Jerusalem is the place where persons ought to worship." (John 4:20) Did Jesus tell the Samaritan woman that God accepts all worship? Or did he say that specific things are required to please God?

² Jesus' startling reply was: "The hour is coming when neither in this mountain nor in Jerusalem will you people worship the Father." (John 4:21) The Samaritans had long feared Jehovah and had worshiped other gods on Mount Gerizim. (2 Kings 17:33) Now Jesus Christ said that neither that place nor Jerusalem would be important in true worship.

WORSHIP WITH SPIRIT AND TRUTH

³ Jesus went on to tell the Samaritan woman: "You

---

1. What did a Samaritan woman want to know about worship?
2. In answering the Samaritan woman, what did Jesus say?
3. (a) Why did the Samaritans not really know God? (b) How could faithful Jews and others come to know God?

worship what you do not know; we worship what we know, because salvation originates with the Jews." (John 4:22) The Samaritans had false religious ideas and accepted only the first five books of the Bible as inspired—and these solely in their own recension known as the Samaritan Pentateuch. Therefore, they did not really know God. However, the Jews had been entrusted with Scriptural knowledge. (Romans 3:1, 2) The Scriptures gave faithful Jews and any others who would listen what they needed in order to know God.

[4] Actually, Jesus showed that both Jews and Samaritans would have to adjust their way of worship so as to please God. He said: "The hour is coming, and it is now, when the true worshipers will worship the Father with spirit and truth, for, indeed, the Father is looking for suchlike ones to worship him. God is a Spirit, and those worshiping him must worship with spirit and truth." (John 4:23, 24) We need to worship God "with spirit," motivated by hearts full of faith and love. It is possible to worship God 'with truth' by studying his Word, the Bible, and by worshiping him according to his revealed truth. Are you eager to do that?

[5] Jesus emphasized that God wants *true* worship. This shows that there are forms of worship unacceptable to Jehovah. To worship God means to give him reverent honor and to render sacred service to him. If you wanted to show honor to a powerful ruler, likely you would be eager to serve him and do what would please him. Surely, then, we want to please God. Rather than merely say, 'My religion suits me,' we therefore

---

4. According to Jesus, what would both Jews and Samaritans need to do if their worship was to be acceptable to God?

5. (a) What does "worship" mean? (b) What must we do if we want God to accept our worship?

need to make sure that our worship meets God's requirements.

DOING THE WILL OF THE FATHER

⁶ Let us read Matthew 7:21-23 and see if we can isolate a crucial factor that determines whether all worship is acceptable to God. Jesus said: "Not everyone saying to me, 'Lord, Lord,' will enter into the kingdom of the heavens, but the one doing the will of my Father who is in the heavens will. Many will say to me in that day, 'Lord, Lord, did we not prophesy in your name, and expel demons [wicked spirit creatures] in your name, and perform many powerful works in your name?' And yet then I will confess to them: I never knew you! Get away from me, you workers of lawlessness."

⁷ Acknowledging Jesus Christ as Lord is essential in true worship. But something would be missing in the worship of many of those claiming to be Jesus' disciples. He said that some would perform "powerful works," such as supposed miraculous healings. However, they would fail to do what Jesus said is vital. They would not be "doing the will of [his] Father." If we want to please God, we must learn what the will of the Father is and then do it.

ACCURATE KNOWLEDGE—A PROTECTION

⁸ Doing God's will requires an accurate knowledge of both Jehovah God and Jesus Christ. Such knowledge leads to everlasting life. Surely, then, all of us will want

---

6, 7. Why does Jesus not acknowledge some who claim to be his disciples?

8. If we are to do God's will, what is required, and what mistaken views must we avoid?

to take seriously the matter of gaining accurate knowledge from God's Word, the Bible. Some say that there is no need for concern as long as we are sincere and zealous in our worship. Others claim, 'The less you know, the less is expected of you.' Yet, the Bible encourages us to increase in the knowledge of God and his purposes. —Ephesians 4:13; Philippians 1:9; Colossians 1:9.

⁹ Such knowledge is a protection against contamination of our worship. The apostle Paul spoke of a certain spirit creature who pretends to be "an angel of light." (2 Corinthians 11:14) Thus disguised, this spirit creature—Satan—tries to mislead us into doing things contrary to God's will. Other spirit creatures associated with Satan have also been polluting people's worship, for Paul said: "The things which the nations sacrifice they sacrifice to demons, and not to God." (1 Corinthians 10:20) Likely, many have thought they were worshiping in the right way, although they were not doing what God wanted. They were being misled into unclean false worship. We will learn more about Satan and the demons later, but these enemies of God have definitely been polluting mankind's worship.

¹⁰ If you knew that someone had deliberately poisoned your water supply, would you go on drinking from it? Surely, you would take immediate action to find a source of safe, pure water. Well, an accurate knowledge of God's Word equips us to identify true religion and to reject impurities that make worship unacceptable to God.

---

9. How does accurate knowledge protect us, and why do we need such protection?

10. What would you do if someone deliberately poisoned your water supply, and what does accurate knowledge of God's Word equip us to do?

COMMANDS OF MEN AS DOCTRINES

[11] When Jesus was on earth, many Jews did not act in accord with accurate knowledge of God. They therefore lost the opportunity to have a clean standing before Jehovah. Concerning them, Paul wrote: "I bear them witness that they have a zeal for God; but not according to accurate knowledge." (Romans 10:2) They decided for themselves how to worship God instead of listening to what he said.

[12] The Israelites originally practiced God-given pure religion, but it became contaminated with teachings and philosophies of men. (Jeremiah 8:8, 9; Malachi 2: 8, 9; Luke 11:52) Although the Jewish religious leaders known as Pharisees *thought* their worship was acceptable to God, Jesus told them: "Isaiah aptly prophesied about you hypocrites, as it is written, 'This people honor me with their lips, but their hearts are far removed from me. It is in vain that they keep worshiping me, because they teach as doctrines commands of men.'" —Mark 7:6, 7.

[13] Is it possible that we might do as the Pharisees did? This could happen if we followed religious traditions handed down to us instead of examining what God has said about worship. Warning of this very real danger, Paul wrote: "The inspired utterance says definitely that in later periods of time some will fall away from the faith, paying attention to misleading inspired utterances and teachings of demons." (1 Timothy 4:1) So it is not enough merely to assume that our worship pleases God. Like the Samaritan woman who met Jesus, we may have inherited our way of worship from our par-

11. What was wrong with the worship of many Jews?
12. What contaminated Israel's worship, and with what result?
13. How might we do as the Pharisees did?

ents. But we need to be certain that we are doing things that meet with God's approval.

GUARD AGAINST OFFENDING GOD

¹⁴ Unless we are careful, we may do something unacceptable to God. For example, the apostle John fell at the feet of an angel "to worship him." But the angel warned: "Be careful! Do not do that! All I am is a fellow slave of you and of your brothers who have the work of witnessing to Jesus. Worship God." (Revelation 19:10) Do you therefore see the need to make sure that your worship is not contaminated by any kind of idolatry? —1 Corinthians 10:14.

¹⁵ When some Christians began to practice religious customs that did not please God, Paul asked: "How is it that you are turning back again to the weak and beggarly elementary things and want to slave for them over again? You are scrupulously observing days and months and seasons and years. I fear for you, that somehow I have toiled to no purpose respecting you." (Galatians 4:8-11) Those individuals had gained a knowledge of God but later erred by observing religious customs and holy days that were unacceptable to Jehovah. As Paul said, we need to "keep on making sure of what is acceptable to the Lord."—Ephesians 5:10.

¹⁶ We must make sure that we avoid religious holidays and other customs that violate God's principles. (1 Thessalonians 5:21) For instance, Jesus said of his followers: "They are no part of the world, just as I am no part of the world." (John 17:16) Is your religion

---

14, 15. Even if we have some knowledge of God's will, why do we need to be careful?

16. How do John 17:16 and 1 Peter 4:3 help us to decide if holidays and customs please God?

involved in ceremonies and holidays that violate the
principle of neutrality toward this world's affairs? Or do
adherents of your religion sometimes share in customs
and festivals that may involve conduct matching that
described by the apostle Peter? He wrote: "The time
that has passed by is sufficient for you to have worked
out the will of the nations when you proceeded in deeds
of loose conduct, lusts, excesses with wine, revelries,
drinking matches, and illegal idolatries."—1 Peter 4:3.

[17] The apostle John emphasized the need to avoid any
practices that reflect the spirit of the ungodly world
around us. John wrote: "Do not be loving either the
world or the things in the world. If anyone loves the
world, the love of the Father is not in him; because
everything in the world—the desire of the flesh and
the desire of the eyes and the showy display of one's
means of life—does not originate with the Father, but
originates with the world. Furthermore, the world is
passing away and so is its desire, but he that does the
will of God remains forever." (1 John 2:15-17) Did you
notice that those who 'do the will of God' will remain
forever? Yes, if we do God's will and avoid activities that
reflect this world's spirit, we can have the hope of everlasting life!

KEEP GOD'S HIGH STANDARDS

[18] God wants as his worshipers those who comply
with his high moral standards. Some in ancient Corinth
mistakenly thought that God would tolerate immoral behavior. We can see how wrong they were by reading 1 Corinthians 6:9, 10. If we are to worship God ac-

17. Why should we avoid anything that reflects the spirit of the
world?
18. How were some Corinthians mistaken about conduct, and
what should we learn from this?

ceptably, we must please him in word and deed. Is your form of worship enabling you to do that?—Matthew 15:8; 23:1-3.

[19] Our dealings with other people should also reflect God's standards. Jesus Christ encouraged us to treat others as we would like to have them treat us, for this is part of true worship. (Matthew 7:12) Note what he also said about displaying brotherly love: "By this all will know that you are my disciples, if you have love among yourselves." (John 13:35) Jesus' disciples must love one another and do what is good toward fellow worshipers and others.—Galatians 6:10.

WHOLE-SOULED WORSHIP

[20] In your heart, you may want to worship God acceptably. If so, you must have Jehovah's view of worship. The disciple James emphasized that it is God's viewpoint that is important, not ours. James said: "The form of worship that is clean and undefiled from the standpoint of our God and Father is this: to look after orphans and widows in their tribulation, and to keep oneself without spot from the world." (James 1:27) With a desire to please God, each of us needs to examine our worship to make sure that it is not contaminated by ungodly practices or that we are not omitting something that he considers vital.—James 1:26.

[21] Only clean, whole-souled worship pleases Jehovah. (Matthew 22:37; Colossians 3:23) When the nation of Israel gave God less than that, he said: "A son, for his part, honors a father; and a servant, his grand master. So if I am a father, where is the honor to me? And if I

---

19. How does true worship affect our treatment of others?

20, 21. (a) What kind of worship does God require? (b) Why did Jehovah reject Israel's worship in Malachi's day?

am a grand master, where is the fear of me?" They were offending God by offering him blind, lame, and sick animals in sacrifice, and he rejected such acts of worship. (Malachi 1:6-8) Jehovah is worthy of the purest form of worship and accepts nothing less than exclusive devotion.—Exodus 20:5; Proverbs 3:9; Revelation 4:11.

²² The Samaritan woman who spoke with Jesus was seemingly interested in worshiping God in the divinely approved way. If that is our desire, we will avoid all contaminating teachings and practices. (2 Corinthians 6:14-18) Instead, we will exert ourselves to get an accurate knowledge of God and do his will. We will adhere closely to his requirements for acceptable worship. (1 Timothy 2:3, 4) Jehovah's Witnesses are striving to do just that, and they warmly urge you to share with them in worshiping God "with spirit and truth." (John 4:24) Jesus said: "The Father is looking for suchlike ones to worship him." (John 4:23) It is hoped that you are such a person. Like that Samaritan woman, undoubtedly you would like to have everlasting life. (John 4:13-15) But you see people grow old and die. The next chapter explains why.

22. If we want God to accept our worship, what will we avoid, and what will we do?

TEST YOUR KNOWLEDGE

As shown at John 4:23, 24, what worship does God accept?

•

How can we determine whether God is pleased with certain customs and festivals?

•

What are some requirements for acceptable worship?

CHAPTER 6

WHY DO WE GROW OLD AND DIE?

SCIENTISTS do not know why humans grow old and die. It seems that our cells should keep on being renewed and that we should live forever. The book *Hyojun Soshikigaku* (Standard Histology) says: "It is a great mystery how the aging of cells is related to the aging and death of an individual." Many scientists believe that there is a "natural, inherent" limit to life. Do you think they are right?

² Humans have always yearned for longevity and have even tried to attain immortality. Since the fourth century B.C.E., drugs supposedly designed to make immortality possible attracted the attention of Chinese nobles. Some later Chinese emperors tried so-called elixirs of life—made from mercury—and died! Around the globe, people believe that death is not the end of their existence. Buddhists, Hindus, Muslims, and others all have bright hopes of a life after death. In Christendom, many envisage an afterlife of heavenly bliss.

³ Concepts of happiness after death reflect a longing for eternal life. "Even time indefinite he has put in their heart," says the Bible concerning the idea of eternity

1. What have scientists been unable to explain about human life?
2. What have some done because of life's fleeting nature?
3. (a) Why do humans long for eternal life? (b) What questions about death need to be answered?

that God implanted in us. (Ecclesiastes 3:11) He created the first humans with the prospect that they could live forever on earth. (Genesis 2:16, 17) Why, then, do humans die? How was death introduced into the world? The knowledge of God sheds light on these questions. —Psalm 119:105.

A SINISTER PLOT

4 A criminal tries to cover his tracks. This has also been true of the one responsible for a crime that has resulted in the death of billions. He has maneuvered things to shroud human death in mystery. Jesus Christ identified this criminal when He told those seeking to kill Him: "You are from your father the Devil, and you wish to do the desires of your father. That one was a manslayer when he began, and he did not stand fast in the truth, because truth is not in him."—John 8:31, 40, 44.

5 Yes, the Devil is a malicious "manslayer." The Bible reveals that he is a real person, not just the evil in someone's heart. (Matthew 4:1-11) Although created as a righteous angel, "he did not stand fast in the truth." How fitting it is that he is named Satan the Devil! (Revelation 12:9) He is called "Satan," or "resister," because he has opposed and resisted Jehovah. This criminal is also called "Devil," meaning "slanderer," for he has blasphemously misrepresented God.

6 What motivated Satan to rebel against God? Greed. He greedily coveted the worship Jehovah received from humans. The Devil did not reject the desire to receive

---

4. How did Jesus identify the criminal responsible for human death?
5. (a) What was the origin of the one who became Satan the Devil? (b) What do the words "Satan" and "Devil" mean?
6. Why did Satan rebel against God?

such worship, which rightly belonged only to the Creator. (Compare Ezekiel 28:12-19.) Instead, the angel who became Satan nurtured this greedy desire until it became fertile and gave birth to sin.—James 1:14, 15.

[7] We have identified the culprit whose criminal act has led to the death of humans. But what is the specific cause of human death? The Bible says: "The sting producing death is sin." (1 Corinthians 15:56) And what is sin? To understand this word, let us consider the meaning it carried in the original languages of the Bible. The Hebrew and Greek verbs commonly translated "to sin" mean "to miss" in the sense of missing a mark or not reaching a goal. What mark do all of us miss? The mark of perfect obedience to God. How, though, was sin introduced into the world?

HOW THE PLOT WAS CARRIED OUT

[8] Satan carefully laid out a plot that he thought would lead to his ruling all humans and receiving their worship. He decided to induce the first human couple, Adam and Eve, to sin against God. Jehovah had given our first parents knowledge that would have led to life everlasting. They knew that their Creator was good because he had placed them in the beautiful garden of Eden. Adam especially felt the goodness of his heavenly Father when God gave him a beautiful and helpful wife. (Genesis 1:26, 29; 2:7-9, 18-23) The continued life of the first human pair depended on obedience to God.

[9] God commanded Adam: "From every tree of the garden you may eat to satisfaction. But as for the tree of

7. (a) What causes human death? (b) What is sin?

8. How did Satan try to gain the worship of humans?

9. What command did God give the first human, and why was this reasonable?

the knowledge of good and bad you must not eat from it, for in the day you eat from it you will positively die." (Genesis 2:16, 17) As the Creator, Jehovah God had the right to set moral standards and to define what was good and what was bad for his creatures. His command was reasonable because Adam and Eve were free to eat fruit from all the other trees in the garden. They could show their appreciation for Jehovah's rightful rulership by obeying this law instead of proudly setting their own moral standards.

¹⁰ The Devil schemed to draw the first humans away from God. To lure them into taking his side, Satan lied. Using a serpent, much as a ventriloquist uses a dummy, the Devil asked Eve: "Is it really so that God said you must not eat from every tree of the garden?" When Eve cited God's command, Satan declared: "You positively will not die." He then imputed bad motives to Jehovah by saying: "God knows that in the very day of your eating from it your eyes are bound to be opened and you are bound to be like God, knowing good and bad." (Genesis 3:1-5) The Devil thus suggested that God was withholding something good. What a slanderous assault on the truthful, loving heavenly Father, Jehovah!

¹¹ Eve looked at the tree again, and its fruit now seemed especially desirable. So she took the fruit and ate it. Later, her husband willfully joined her in this sinful act of disobedience to God. (Genesis 3:6) Although Eve was deceived, both she and Adam supported Satan's scheme to rule the human race. In effect, they became his accomplices.—Romans 6:16; 1 Timothy 2:14.

---

10. (a) How did Satan approach humans to draw them to his side? (b) What motives did Satan impute to Jehovah? (c) What do *you* think about Satan's attack on God?

11. How did Adam and Eve become Satan's accomplices?

¹² Adam and Eve had to face the consequences of their actions. They did not become like God, with special knowledge. Instead, they felt ashamed and hid themselves. Jehovah called Adam to account and pronounced this sentence: "In the sweat of your face you will eat bread until you return to the ground, for out of it you were taken. For dust you are and to dust you will return." (Genesis 3:19) "In the day" that our first parents ate from the tree of the knowledge of good and bad, they were sentenced by God and died from his standpoint. Then they were expelled from Paradise and began their descent into physical death.

HOW SIN AND DEATH SPREAD

¹³ Satan had apparently succeeded in his scheme to receive human veneration. Yet, he could not keep his worshipers alive. When sin started to work in the first human couple, they could no longer pass on perfection to their offspring. Like an inscription carved in stone, sin was deeply engraved into the genes of our first parents. Thus, they could produce only imperfect offspring. Since all their children were conceived after Adam and Eve sinned, their offspring inherited sin and death. —Psalm 51:5; Romans 5:12.

¹⁴ Today, however, many do not think that they are sinners. In some parts of the world, the concept of inherited sin is generally unknown. But that is no proof that sin does not exist. A boy with a dirty face may claim that he is clean, and may be convinced otherwise only after he looks into a mirror. The ancient Israelites were

12. What resulted from the human rebellion against God?
13. How did sin spread to all the human race?
14. (a) To whom might we liken those who deny their sin?
(b) How were the Israelites made aware of their sinfulness?

like such a boy when they received God's Law through His prophet Moses. The Law made it plain that sin existed. "Really I would not have come to know sin if it had not been for the Law," explains the apostle Paul. (Romans 7:7-12) Like the boy looking into a mirror, by using the Law to look at themselves, the Israelites could see that they were unclean in Jehovah's eyes.

¹⁵ By looking into the mirror of God's Word and noting its standards, we can see that we are imperfect. (James 1:23-25) For example, consider what Jesus Christ told his disciples about loving God and their neighbor, as recorded at Matthew 22:37-40. How often humans miss the mark in these areas! Many do not feel even a twinge of conscience over failing to show love for God or for their neighbors.—Luke 10:29-37.

BEWARE OF SATAN'S TACTICS!

¹⁶ Satan seeks to cause us to practice sin willfully. (1 John 3:8) Is there any way to avoid being a victim of his schemes? Yes, but this requires that we fight inclinations toward willful sin. This is not easy because our inborn tendency to sin is very strong. (Ephesians 2:3) Paul had to put up a real struggle. Why? Because sin resided in him. If we want God's approval, we too must fight the sinful tendencies within us.—Romans 7:14-24; 2 Corinthians 5:10.

¹⁷ Since Satan constantly looks for opportunities to lure us into breaking God's laws, our fight against sin is not easy. (1 Peter 5:8) Showing concern for fellow

---

15. What is revealed by looking into the mirror of God's Word?

16. What can we do to avoid becoming a victim of Satan's schemes, and why is this difficult?

17. What makes the fight against our sinful tendencies more difficult?

Christians, Paul said: "I am afraid that somehow, as the serpent seduced Eve by its cunning, your minds might be corrupted away from the sincerity and the chastity that are due the Christ." (2 Corinthians 11:3) Satan uses similar tactics today. He tries to sow seeds of doubt about Jehovah's goodness and the benefits of obeying God's commands. The Devil tries to take advantage of our inherited sinful tendencies and have us pursue a course of pride, greed, hatred, and prejudice.

¹⁸ One of the devices the Devil uses against us is the world, which is lying in his power. (1 John 5:19) If we are not careful, corrupt and dishonest people in the world around us will pressure us into a sinful course that violates God's moral standards. (1 Peter 4:3-5) Many ignore God's laws and even brush aside the proddings of their conscience, eventually rendering it insensitive. (Romans 2:14, 15; 1 Timothy 4:1, 2) Some gradually adopt a course that even their imperfect conscience formerly did not permit them to take.—Romans 1: 24-32; Ephesians 4:17-19.

¹⁹ Living a clean life is an achievement in this world. To please our Creator, however, more is required. We must also have faith in God and feel a responsibility toward him. (Hebrews 11:6) "If one knows how to do what is right and yet does not do it, it is a sin for him," wrote the disciple James. (James 4:17) Yes, deliberately ignoring God and his commandments is itself a form of sin.

²⁰ Satan is very likely to stimulate opposition to your pursuit of the knowledge of God through your study

18. How does Satan use the world to promote sin?
19. Why is it not enough just to live a clean life?
20. How might Satan try to prevent you from doing what is right, but what will help you to resist such pressures?

of the Bible. It is sincerely hoped that you will not let such pressures prevent you from practicing what is right. (John 16:2) Though many rulers put faith in Jesus during his ministry, they did not confess him because they were fearful of being shunned in their community. (John 12:42, 43) Satan ruthlessly tries to intimidate anyone seeking the knowledge of God. However, you should always remember and appreciate the wonderful things Jehovah has done. You may even be able to help opposers to gain the same appreciation.

²¹ As long as we are imperfect, we will sin. (1 John 1:8) Nevertheless, we have help in fighting this battle. Yes, it is possible to come off victorious in our fight against the wicked one, Satan the Devil. (Romans 5:21) At the end of Jesus' ministry on earth, he encouraged his followers with these words: "In the world you are having tribulation, but take courage! I have conquered the world." (John 16:33) Even for imperfect humans, it is possible to conquer the world with God's help. Satan has no hold on those who oppose him and 'subject themselves to God.' (James 4:7; 1 John 5:18) As we shall see, God has provided a way out of bondage to sin and death.

21. How may we conquer the world and our own sinful tendencies?

TEST YOUR KNOWLEDGE

Who is Satan the Devil?
•
Why do humans grow old and die?
•
What is sin?
•
How does Satan draw people into
willful sin against God?

CHAPTER 7

WHAT GOD HAS DONE TO SAVE MANKIND

ONE spring afternoon nearly 2,000 years ago, a Roman centurion watched three men die slow, agonizing deaths. That soldier especially noted one of them—Jesus Christ. Jesus had been nailed to a wooden stake. The midday sky blackened as the moment of his death approached. When he died, the earth shook violently, and the soldier exclaimed: "Certainly this man was God's Son."—Mark 15:39.

² God's Son! That soldier was right. He had just witnessed the most important event ever to occur on the earth. On earlier occasions, God himself had called Jesus his beloved Son. (Matthew 3:17; 17:5) Why had Jehovah allowed his Son to die? Because this was God's means of saving mankind from sin and death.

CHOSEN FOR A SPECIAL PURPOSE

³ As we have previously learned in this book, Jesus had a prehuman existence. He is called God's "only-begotten Son" because Jehovah created him directly. God thereafter used Jesus to bring all other things into existence. (John 3:18; Colossians 1:16) Jesus was especially fond of humankind. (Proverbs 8:30, 31) No wonder Jehovah

1, 2. (a) How did a Roman centurion come to appreciate who God's Son is? (b) Why did Jehovah allow Jesus to die?
3. Why was it fitting that God's only-begotten Son be chosen for a special purpose regarding mankind?

chose his only-begotten Son to serve a special purpose when mankind came under the condemnation of death!

⁴ When pronouncing sentence on Adam, Eve, and Satan in the garden of Eden, God spoke of the future Rescuer as a "seed." This Seed, or offspring, would come to undo the terrible ills that Satan the Devil, "the original serpent," had brought about. In fact, the promised Seed would crush Satan and all those who followed him. —Genesis 3:15; 1 John 3:8; Revelation 12:9.

⁵ Over the centuries, God gradually revealed more about the Seed, also called the Messiah. As shown in the chart on page 37, numerous prophecies gave details about many aspects of his life on earth. For instance, he was to endure terrible mistreatment in order to fulfill his role in God's purpose.—Isaiah 53:3-5.

WHY THE MESSIAH WOULD DIE

⁶ The prophecy recorded at Daniel 9:24-26 foretold that the Messiah—God's Anointed One—would fulfill a great purpose. He would come to earth "to terminate the transgression, and to finish off sin, and to make atonement for error, and to bring in righteousness" forever. The Messiah would remove the condemnation of death from faithful mankind. But how would he do this? The prophecy explains that he would be "cut off," or put to death.

⁷ The ancient Israelites were familiar with the idea of atonement for error. In their worship under the Law that God gave them through Moses, they regularly offered up animal sacrifices. These reminded the people of Israel

---

4, 5. Before Jesus came to the earth, what did the Bible reveal about the Messianic Seed?

6. According to Daniel 9:24-26, what would the Messiah accomplish, and how?

7. Why did the Jews offer up animal sacrifices, and what did these foreshadow?

that humans need something to atone for, or cover, their sins. The apostle Paul summarized the principle in this way: "Unless blood is poured out no forgiveness takes place." (Hebrews 9:22) Christians are not under the Mosaic Law with its requirements, such as sacrifices. (Romans 10:4; Colossians 2:16, 17) They also know that animal sacrifices cannot provide permanent and complete forgiveness of sins. Instead, these sacrificial offerings foreshadowed a far more valuable sacrifice—that of the Messiah, or Christ. (Hebrews 10:4, 10; compare Galatians 3:24.) Yet, you may ask, 'Was it really necessary for the Messiah to die?'

[8] Yes, the Messiah had to die if mankind was to be saved. To understand why, we must think back to the garden of Eden and try to grasp the enormity of what Adam and Eve lost when they rebelled against God. Eternal life had been set before them! As children of God, they also enjoyed a direct relationship with him. But when they rejected Jehovah's rulership, they lost all of that and brought sin and death upon the human race.—Romans 5:12.

[9] It was as though our first parents had squandered a vast fortune, plunging themselves into a pit of debt. Adam and Eve passed that debt on to their offspring. Because we were not born perfect and sinless, every one of us is sinful and dying. When we get sick or say something hurtful that we wish we could take back, we are experiencing the effects of our inherited debt—human imperfection. (Romans 7:21-25) Our only hope lies in regaining what Adam lost. However, we cannot earn perfect human life. Since all imperfect humans commit sin, all of us earn death, not life.—Romans 6:23.

[10] Yet, could something be offered in exchange for the

8, 9. What precious things did Adam and Eve lose, and how did their actions affect their descendants?
10. What was needed to buy back what Adam lost?

life that Adam forfeited? God's standard of justice demands balance, "soul for soul." (Exodus 21:23) So a life had to be offered to pay for the life that was lost. Not just any life would suffice. Psalm 49:7, 8 says of imperfect humans: "Not one of them can by any means redeem even a brother, nor give to God a ransom for him; (and the redemption price of their soul is so precious that it has ceased to time indefinite)." Is the situation therefore hopeless? No, indeed.

[11] In the Hebrew language, the word "ransom" signifies the sum paid to redeem a captive and also denotes *equivalency*. Only a man with perfect human life could offer up the equivalent of what Adam lost. After Adam, the only perfect man born on earth was Jesus Christ. Hence, the Bible calls Jesus "the last Adam" and assures us that Christ "gave himself a corresponding ransom for all." (1 Corinthians 15:45; 1 Timothy 2:5, 6) Whereas Adam passed death on to his children, Jesus' legacy is life eternal. First Corinthians 15:22 explains: "Just as in Adam all are dying, so also in the Christ all will be made alive." Appropriately, then, Jesus is called "Eternal Father."—Isaiah 9:6, 7.

HOW THE RANSOM WAS PAID

[12] In the fall of 29 C.E., Jesus went to his relative John to be baptized and thereby present himself to carry out God's will. On that occasion Jehovah anointed Jesus with holy spirit. Jesus thus became the Messiah, or Christ, the one anointed by God. (Matthew 3:16, 17) Then Jesus embarked on his three-and-a-half-year ministry. He traveled throughout his homeland, preaching about God's Kingdom and gathering faithful followers.

---

11. (a) What does the word "ransom" signify in Hebrew? (b) Who alone could redeem mankind, and why?

12. When did Jesus become the Messiah, and what life course did he thereafter pursue?

However, as foretold, opposition to him soon mounted
—Psalm 118:22; Acts 4:8-11.

¹³ Jesus courageously exposed the hypocrisy of the re-
ligious leaders, and they sought his death. They eventually hatched an ugly plot that involved betrayal, improper
arrest, an illegal trial, and a false charge of sedition. Jesus
was struck, spat upon, ridiculed, and beaten with a whip
designed to tear his flesh. The Roman governor Pontius
Pilate then sentenced him to death on a torture stake.
He was nailed to a wooden pole and hung there upright.
Each breath was excruciating, and it took hours for him
to die. Throughout that ordeal, Jesus maintained perfect
integrity to God.

¹⁴ Thus, it was on Nisan 14, 33 C.E., that Jesus gave
his life as "a ransom in exchange for many." (Mark 10:
45; 1 Timothy 2:5, 6) From heaven, Jehovah could see his
dear Son suffer and die. Why did God allow such a terrible thing to happen? He did so because he loved humankind. Jesus said: "God loved the world so much that he
gave his only-begotten Son, in order that everyone exercising faith in him might not be destroyed but have everlasting life." (John 3:16) The death of Jesus also teaches
us that Jehovah is a God of perfect justice. (Deuteronomy 32:4) Some might wonder why God did not waive his
principles of justice that require soul for soul and ignore
the price of Adam's sinful course. The reason is that Jehovah always abides by his laws and upholds them, even
at great cost to himself.

¹⁵ Jehovah's justice also required that Jesus' death have
a happy outcome. After all, would there be justice in allowing faithful Jesus to sleep forever in death? Of course
not! The Hebrew Scriptures had prophesied that God's

---

13. What events led up to Jesus' death as an integrity keeper?
14. Why did God allow his Son to suffer and die?
15. Since it would have been unjust to allow Jesus' existence to
end permanently, what did Jehovah do?

loyal one would not remain in the grave. (Psalm 16:1(
Acts 13:35) He slept in death for parts of three days, an
then Jehovah God resurrected him to life as a might
spirit being.—1 Peter 3:18.

¹⁶ At his death, Jesus surrendered his human life for a
time. Upon being raised to life in heaven, he became :
life-giving spirit. Moreover, when Jesus ascended to th
holiest place in the universe, he was reunited with hi
dear Father and formally presented to Him the value o
his perfect human life. (Hebrews 9:23-28) The value o
that precious life could then be applied in behalf of obe
dient mankind. What does that mean for you?

CHRIST'S RANSOM AND YOU

¹⁷ Consider three ways in which Christ's ransom sacri
fice benefits you even now. First, it brings *forgiveness o
sins.* Through faith in the shed blood of Jesus, we hav
"the release by ransom," yes, "the forgiveness of our tres
passes." (Ephesians 1:7) So even if we have committec
a serious sin, we can ask God for forgiveness in Jesus
name. If we are truly repentant, Jehovah applies to u:
the value of his Son's ransom sacrifice. God forgives us
granting us the blessing of a good conscience, instead o
exacting the penalty of death that we incur by sinning
—Acts 3:19; 1 Peter 3:21.

¹⁸ Second, Christ's ransom sacrifice provides the basis
of our *hope for the future.* In vision, the apostle John saw
that "a great crowd, which no man was able to number"
would survive the coming cataclysmic end of this system
of things. Why will they survive when God destroys so
many others? An angel told John that the great crowd had

16. What did Jesus do upon returning to heaven?
17. How can we avail ourselves of forgiveness on the basis of
Christ's ransom sacrifice?
18. In what way does Jesus' sacrifice provide us with hope?

washed their robes and made them white in the blood of the Lamb," Jesus Christ. (Revelation 7:9, 14) As long as we exercise faith in the shed blood of Jesus Christ and live in harmony with divine requirements, we will be clean in God's sight and will have the hope of everlasting life.

[19] Third, the ransom sacrifice is the ultimate *proof of Jehovah's love*. Christ's death embodied the two greatest acts of love in the history of the universe: (1) God's love in sending his Son to die in our behalf; (2) Jesus' love in willingly offering himself as a ransom. (John 15:13; Romans 5:8) If we truly exercise faith, this love applies to each and every one of us. The apostle Paul said: "The Son of God . . . loved me and handed himself over for me." —Galatians 2:20; Hebrews 2:9; 1 John 4:9, 10.

[20] Therefore, let us show our gratitude for the love displayed by God and Christ by exercising faith in Jesus' ransom sacrifice. Doing so leads to everlasting life. (John 3:36) Yet, our salvation is not the most important reason for Jesus' life and death on earth. No, his primary concern was an even greater issue, a universal one. As we shall see in the next chapter, that issue touches all of us because it shows why God has allowed wickedness and suffering to persist so long in this world.

9. How does Christ's sacrifice prove that he and his Father love you?

20. Why should we exercise faith in Jesus' ransom sacrifice?

TEST YOUR KNOWLEDGE

Why did Jesus have to die to save mankind?

•

How was the ransom paid?

•

In what ways do you
benefit from the ransom?

WHY DOES GOD PERMIT SUFFERING?

WHEN disasters strike, destroying property and claiming lives, many cannot understand why such terrible things happen. Others are troubled by the extent, cruelty, and wantonness of crime and violence. You too may have wondered, 'Why does God permit suffering?'

1, 2. How do people often react to human suffering?

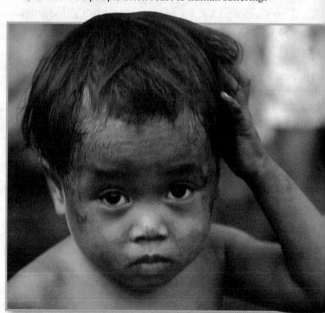

² Because they have found no satisfactory answer to this question, many have lost faith in God. They feel that he is not interested in mankind. Others who accept suffering as a fact of life become embittered and blame God for all the evil in human society. If you have had such feelings, doubtless you will be very interested in the Bible's statements on these matters.

SUFFERING NOT FROM GOD

³ The Bible assures us that the suffering we see around us is not caused by Jehovah God. For instance, the Christian disciple James wrote: "When under trial, let no one say: 'I am being tried by God.' For with evil things God cannot be tried nor does he himself try anyone." (James 1:13) That being so, God could not have caused the numerous hardships plaguing mankind. He does not bring trials upon people to make them fit for life in heaven, nor does he make people suffer for evil deeds they supposedly committed in a past life.—Romans 6:7.

⁴ In addition, even though many terrible things have been done in the name of God or of Christ, there is nothing in the Bible to suggest that either of them has ever approved of such actions. God and Christ have nothing to do with those who claim to serve them but who cheat and swindle, kill and plunder, and do many other things that cause human suffering. In fact, "the way of the wicked one is something detestable to Jehovah." God "is far away from the wicked ones."—Proverbs 15:9, 29.

⁵ The Bible describes Jehovah as being "very tender in

affection and merciful." (James 5:11) It proclaims that
"Jehovah is a lover of justice." (Psalm 37:28; Isaiah 61:8)
He is not vindictive. He compassionately cares for his
creatures and gives all of them what is best for their
well-being. (Acts 14:16, 17) Jehovah has done that from
the very origin of life on the earth.

A PERFECT BEGINNING

⁶ All of us are accustomed to seeing and feeling pain
and suffering. It may therefore be hard to imagine a time
without suffering, but that was how things were at the
beginning of human history. Even the legends of some
nations allude to such a happy start. In Greek mythol-
ogy, the first of the "Five Ages of Man" was called the
"Golden Age." In it humans lived happy lives, free from
toil, pain, and the ravages of old age. The Chinese say
that during the reign of the mythological Yellow Em-
peror (Huang-Ti), people lived in peace, enjoying harmony even with the elements and the wild beasts. Persians, Egyptians, Tibetans, Peruvians, and Mexicans all
have legends about a time of happiness and perfection
at the beginning of mankind's history.

⁷ The myths of the nations merely echo the oldest
written record of human history, the Bible. It informs
us that God placed the first human pair, Adam and Eve,
in a paradise called the garden of Eden and commanded
them: "Be fruitful and become many and fill the earth
and subdue it." (Genesis 1:28) Our first parents enjoyed
perfection and had the prospect of seeing the whole
earth become a paradise occupied by a perfect human
family living in lasting peace and happiness. That was
God's purpose in creating the earth and humankind.
—Isaiah 45:18.

6. How do some legends allude to mankind's early history?
7. Why did God create the earth and humankind?

A MALICIOUS CHALLENGE

⁸ To remain in God's favor, Adam and Eve would have to refrain from eating from "the tree of the knowledge of good and bad." (Genesis 2:16, 17) If they had obeyed Jehovah's law, there would have been no suffering to mar human life. By obeying God's command, they would have demonstrated their love for Jehovah and their loyalty to him. (1 John 5:3) But as we learned in Chapter 6, things did not turn out that way. Urged by Satan, Eve ate fruit from that tree. Later, Adam also partook of the forbidden fruit.

⁹ Do you see the seriousness of what happened? Satan was attacking Jehovah's position as the Most High. By saying, "You positively will not die," the Devil contradicted God's words, "You will positively die." Satan's further words implied that Jehovah was keeping Adam and Eve ignorant of the possibility of becoming like God, thus not needing Him to decide what was good and bad. Satan's challenge therefore brought into question the right and validity of Jehovah's position as the Universal Sovereign.—Genesis 2:17; 3:1-6.

¹⁰ Satan the Devil also insinuated that people would remain obedient to Jehovah only as long as obeying God was to their advantage. In other words, human integrity was brought into question. Satan charged that no human would voluntarily remain loyal to God. This malicious claim by Satan is clearly revealed in the Bible's account about Job, a faithful servant of Jehovah who underwent a great test sometime before 1600 B.C.E. When you read the first two chapters of the book of Job,

8. Adam and Eve were expected to obey what command, but what happened?
9. What issue involving Jehovah did Satan raise?
10. What insinuations did Satan make regarding humans?

you can gain insight into the reason for human suffering and why God permits it.

[11] Job, "a man blameless and upright," came under Satan's attack. First, Satan imputed bad motives to Job by raising the question, "Is it for nothing that Job has feared God?" Then, the Devil cunningly maligned both God and Job by charging that Jehovah had bought Job's loyalty by protecting and blessing him. "But, for a change," Satan challenged Jehovah, "thrust out your hand, please, and touch everything he has and see whether he will not curse you to your very face."—Job 1:8-11.

[12] Was Job serving Jehovah simply because of all the good that he received from God? Could Job's integrity stand up under test? In turn, did Jehovah have enough confidence in his servant to allow him to be tested? These questions could be answered if Jehovah would permit Satan to bring upon Job the severest of tests. Job's faithful course under the test allowed by God, as narrated in the book of Job, proved to be a thorough vindication of Jehovah's righteousness and man's integrity.—Job 42:1, 2, 12.

[13] What happened in the garden of Eden and to the man Job, however, has a deeper implication. The issues Satan raised involve all mankind, including us today. God's name was maligned, and his sovereignty was challenged. The uprightness of God's creation, man, was called into question. These issues had to be settled.

11. What kind of man was Job, but what charge did Satan make?
12. (a) What questions could be answered only if God permitted Satan to test Job? (b) In what did Job's test result?
13. How are we involved in what happened in Eden and to Job?

HOW TO SETTLE THE ISSUES

¹⁴ For the sake of illustration, let us say that you are a loving parent with several children in a happy family. Suppose one of your neighbors spreads lies, accusing you of being a bad parent. What if the neighbor says that your children do not love you, that they stay with you only because they do not know any better, and that they would leave if someone showed them the way. 'Preposterous!' you might say. Yes, but how would you prove it? Some parents might react in rage. Besides creating more problems, such a violent response would lend support to the lies. A satisfying way to deal with such a problem would be to allow opportunity for your

---

14. When confronted with a malicious challenge, what might an accused person do?

accuser to prove his claim and for your children to testify that they sincerely love you.

¹⁵ Jehovah is like the loving parent. Adam and Eve may be compared to the children, and Satan fits the role of the lying neighbor. God wisely did not destroy Satan, Adam, and Eve immediately but permitted these wrongdoers to continue living for a while. This allowed our first parents time to start the human family, and it has given the Devil a chance to prove whether his claim was true so that the issues could be settled. From the start, however, God knew that some humans would be loyal to him and would thus prove Satan a liar. How thankful we are that Jehovah has continued to bless and help those who love him! —2 Chronicles 16:9; Proverbs 15:3.

WHAT HAS BEEN PROVED?

¹⁶ During nearly all human history, Satan has had a free hand to work out his schemes of domination over mankind. Among other things, he has wielded influence over the political powers and has promoted religions that subtly direct worship to him rather than to Jehovah. Thus the Devil has become "the god of this system of things," and he is called "the ruler of this world." (2 Corinthians 4:4; John 12:31) Indeed, "the whole world is lying in the power of the wicked one." (1 John 5:19) Does this mean that Satan has proved his claim that he could draw all mankind away from Jehovah God? Certainly not! While permitting Satan to remain in existence, Jehovah has proceeded to carry out his own purpose. What, then, does the Bible reveal concerning God's permission of wickedness?

---

15. How did Jehovah choose to deal with Satan's challenge?
16. How has the world come to be in Satan's power?

[17] *Wickedness and suffering are not caused by Jehovah.* Since Satan is the ruler of this world and the god of this system of things, he and those on his side are responsible for the present condition of human society and all the misery that mankind has suffered. No one can rightly say that God is the cause of such hardship. —Romans 9:14.

[18] Jehovah's permitting wickedness and suffering has proved that *independence from God has not brought about a better world.* Undeniably, history has been marked by one disaster after another. The reason for this is that humans have chosen to pursue their own independent course and have shown no real regard for God's word and will. When Jehovah's ancient people and their leaders unfaithfully pursued "the popular course" and rejected his word, the results were disastrous. Through his prophet Jeremiah, God told them: "The wise ones have become ashamed. They have become terrified and will be caught. Look! They have rejected the very word of Jehovah, and what wisdom do they have?" (Jeremiah 8:5, 6, 9) Having failed to follow Jehovah's standards, mankind in general has become like a ship without a rudder, tossed about in a turbulent sea.

[19] God's permission of wickedness and suffering has also proved that *Satan has not been able to turn all mankind away from Jehovah.* History shows that there have always been individuals who have remained faithful to God no matter what temptations or adversities were brought upon them. Over the centuries, Jehovah's

---

17. What should we keep in mind regarding the cause of wickedness and suffering?
18. What has Jehovah's permitting wickedness and suffering proved regarding the idea of independence from God?
19. What proof is there that Satan cannot turn all humans against God?

power has been manifested in behalf of his servants, and his name has been declared in all the earth. (Exodus 9:16; 1 Samuel 12:22) Hebrews chapter 11 tells us about a long line of faithful ones, including Abel, Enoch, Noah, Abraham, and Moses. Hebrews 12:1 calls them 'a great cloud of witnesses.' They were examples of unwavering faith in Jehovah. In modern times too, many have given their lives in unbreakable integrity to God. By their faith and love, such individuals prove conclusively that Satan cannot turn all humans against God.

[20] Finally, Jehovah's allowing wickedness and suffering to continue has provided proof that *only Jehovah, the Creator, has the ability and the right to rule over mankind* for their eternal blessing and happiness. For centuries, mankind has tried many forms of government. But what has been the result? The complex problems and crises facing the nations today are ample evidence that truly, as the Bible points out, "man has dominated man to his injury." (Ecclesiastes 8:9) Only Jehovah can come to our rescue and fulfill his original purpose. How will he do this, and when?

[21] Right after Adam and Eve fell victim to Satan's scheme, God announced His purpose regarding a means of salvation. This is what Jehovah proclaimed regarding Satan: "I shall put enmity between you and the woman and between your seed and her seed. He will bruise you in the head and you will bruise him in the heel." (Genesis 3:15) That proclamation guaranteed that the Devil would not be allowed to do his evil deeds forever. As the King of the Messianic Kingdom, the promised Seed, Jesus Christ, will 'bruise Satan in

20. Jehovah's allowing wickedness and suffering to continue has proved what with respect to God and mankind?
21. What will be done to Satan, and who will be used to accomplish this?

the head.' Yes, "shortly," Jesus will crush the rebel Satan!—Romans 16:20.

WHAT WILL YOU DO?

22 Knowing the issues involved, on whose side will you stand? Will you prove by your actions that you are a loyal supporter of Jehovah? Since Satan knows that his time is short, he will do all he can to vent his wrath on those who want to keep integrity to God. (Revelation 12:12) But you can look to God for help because "Jehovah knows how to deliver people of godly devotion out of trial." (2 Peter 2:9) He will not let you be tempted beyond what you can bear, and he will make the way out so that you are able to endure temptations.—1 Corinthians 10:13.

23 Confidently, let us look forward to the time when the King Jesus Christ will take action against Satan and all who follow him. (Revelation 20:1-3) Jesus will do away with all those who share responsibility for the woes and turmoil that mankind has suffered. Until that time, one especially painful form of suffering is the loss of our loved ones in death. Read the next chapter to find out what happens to them.

---

22. (a) What questions must you face? (b) Though Satan vents his wrath on those faithful to God, of what can they be certain?
23. To what can we confidently look forward?

TEST YOUR KNOWLEDGE

How do we know that Jehovah does not cause human suffering?

•

What issues were raised by Satan in Eden and made clear in Job's day?

•

God's permission of suffering has proved what?

CHAPTER 9

WHAT HAPPENS
TO OUR
DEAD LOVED ONES?

"ONE suffers when a loved one dies because death is a loss to a void beyond all understanding." That is what one son said when his father and shortly thereafter his mother died. His pain and sense of deep loss made him feel that he was "drowning emotionally." Perhaps you have suffered in a similar way. You may have wondered where your loved ones are and whether you will ever see them again.

² Some grieving parents have been told, "God picks the most beautiful flowers to take to himself in heaven." Is that really so? Have our dead loved ones gone to a spirit realm? Is it what some call Nirvana, described as a blissful state of being free of all pain and desire? Have those we love passed through a doorway to immortal life in paradise? Or as others claim, is death a fall into never-ending torment for those who have offended God? Can the dead affect our lives? To get truthful answers to such questions, we need to consult God's Word, the Bible.

WHAT IS THE "SPIRIT" IN HUMANS?

³ The ancient Greek philosophers Socrates and Plato

---

1. How do people feel when death strikes a loved one?
2. What perplexing questions arise concerning death?
3. What opinion did Socrates and Plato have regarding the dead, and how does this affect people today?

held that there must be something inherently immortal inside man and woman—a soul that survives death and never really dies. Earth wide, millions believe this today. This belief often engenders as much fear of the dead as it does concern for their welfare. The Bible teaches us something quite different about the dead.

⁴ In considering the condition of the dead, we must remember that our original father, Adam, did not *have* a soul. He *was* a soul. In an awe-inspiring act of creation, God formed man—the soul—from the basic elements of the earth and then breathed into him "the breath of life." Genesis 2:7 tells us: "Jehovah God proceeded to form the man out of dust from the ground and to blow into his nostrils the breath of life, and the man came to be a living soul." Adam's life was sustained by breathing. Yet, more than the blowing of air into man's lungs was involved when God put the breath of life into Adam. The Bible speaks of "the force of life" that is active in earthly living creatures.—Genesis 7:22.

⁵ What is "the force of life"? It is the vital spark of life that God put into the lifeless body of Adam. This force was then sustained by the breathing process. But what is the "spirit" referred to at Psalm 146:4? That verse says of one who dies: "His spirit goes out, he goes back to his ground; in that day his thoughts do perish." When the Bible writers used the word "spirit" in this way, they did not have in mind a disembodied soul that continues living after the body dies.

⁶ The "spirit" that departs from humans at death is the life force that originated with our Creator. (Psalm 36:9;

---

4. (a) What does Genesis tell us about the soul? (b) What did God put into Adam to make him alive?

5, 6. (a) What is "the force of life"? (b) What happens when the "spirit" mentioned at Psalm 146:4 ceases to animate the body?

Acts 17:28) This life force does not have any of the characteristics of the creature it animates, just as electricity does not take on the features of the equipment it powers. When someone dies, the spirit (life force) ceases to animate the body cells, much as a light goes out when the electricity is turned off. When the life force stops sustaining the human body, man—the soul—dies. —Psalm 104:29; Ecclesiastes 12:1, 7.

"TO DUST YOU WILL RETURN"

7 Jehovah clearly explained what death would mean for the sinner Adam. God said: "In the sweat of your face you will eat bread until you return to the ground, for out of it you were taken. For dust you are and to dust you will return." (Genesis 3:19) Adam would return where? To the ground, to the dust from which he had been created. At death Adam would simply cease to exist!

8 In this regard, human death does not differ from that of the animals. They too are souls, and the same spirit, or life force, energizes them. (Genesis 1:24) At Ecclesiastes 3:19, 20, the wise man Solomon tells us: "As the one dies, so the other dies; and they all have but one spirit, so that [in death] there is no superiority of the man over the beast . . . They have all come to be from the dust, and they are all returning to the dust." Man was superior to the beasts in that he was created in God's image, reflecting the qualities of Jehovah. (Genesis 1:26, 27) Yet, at death humans and animals alike return to the dust.

9 Solomon further explained what death means, saying: "The living are conscious that they will die; but as for the dead, they are conscious of nothing at all." Yes, the dead know absolutely nothing. In view of this, Solo-

7. What would happen to Adam if he disobeyed God?
8. As souls, in what way are humans not superior to animals?
9. What is the condition of the dead, and where do they go?

mon urged: "All that your hand finds to do, do with your very power, for there is no work nor devising nor knowledge nor wisdom in Sheol, the place to which you are going." (Ecclesiastes 9:5, 10) Where do the dead go? To Sheol (Hebrew, *she'ohl'*), the common grave of mankind. Our dead loved ones are not conscious of anything. They are not suffering, and they cannot affect us in any way.

¹⁰ Must all of us and our loved ones live only a few years and then cease to exist forever? Not according to the Bible. At the time of Adam's rebellion, Jehovah God immediately instituted arrangements to reverse the terrible consequences of human sin. Death was not part of God's purpose for mankind. (Ezekiel 33:11; 2 Peter 3:9) Hence, death does not have to be final for us or for our loved ones.

"GONE TO REST"

¹¹ It is Jehovah's purpose to rescue us and our dead loved ones from Adamic death. Therefore, God's Word refers to the dead as being asleep. For example, upon learning that his friend Lazarus had died, Jesus Christ told His disciples: "Lazarus our friend has gone to rest, but I am journeying there to awaken him from sleep." Since the disciples did not immediately grasp the meaning of this statement, Jesus said plainly: "Lazarus has died." (John 11:11, 14) Jesus then went to the town of Bethany, where Lazarus' sisters Martha and Mary were mourning their brother's death. When Jesus told Martha, "Your brother will rise," she expressed her faith in God's purpose to reverse the effects of death on the human family. She said: "I know he will rise in the resurrection on the last day."—John 11:23, 24.

10. Why can we say that death does not have to be final?
11. How did Jesus describe the condition of his dead friend Lazarus?

[12] Martha expressed no thought about an immortal soul living on elsewhere after death. She did not believe that Lazarus had already gone to some spirit realm to continue his existence. Martha had faith in the wonderful hope of a *resurrection* from the dead. She understood, not that an immortal soul had departed from the body of Lazarus, but that her dead brother had ceased to exist. The remedy would be the resurrection of her brother.

[13] Jesus Christ is the one empowered by Jehovah God to redeem mankind. (Hosea 13:14) Hence, in response to Martha's statement, Jesus said: "I am the resurrection and the life. He that exercises faith in me, even though he dies, will come to life." (John 11:25) Jesus demonstrated his God-given power in this regard when he went to the tomb of Lazarus, who had been dead for four days, and restored him to life. (John 11:38-44) Just imagine the joy of those who saw this resurrection or others performed by Jesus Christ!—Mark 5:35-42; Luke 7:12-16.

[14] Pause for a moment to consider this: Nobody would need to be resurrected, or brought back to life, if an immortal soul survived death. In fact, it would be no kindness to resurrect someone like Lazarus back to imperfect life on earth if he had already passed on to a wonderful heavenly reward. Actually, the Bible never uses the expression "immortal soul." Instead, the Scriptures say that the sinning human soul does die. (Ezekiel 18:4, 20) So the Bible points to the provision of a resurrection as the real remedy for death.

---

12. What hope did bereaved Martha have regarding the dead?
13. What God-given power does Jesus have, and how did he demonstrate this power?
14. Why are the resurrection and the idea of an immortal soul incompatible?

"ALL THOSE IN THE MEMORIAL TOMBS"

¹⁵ The word that Jesus' disciples used for "resurrection" literally means "raising up" or "standing up." This is a raising up from the lifeless condition of death—as it were, a standing up out of the common grave of mankind. Jehovah God can easily resurrect a person. Why? Because Jehovah is the Originator of life. Today, humans can record the voices and images of men and women on videotape and can replay these recordings after the individuals die. Surely, then, our almighty Creator can record the details of any individual and resurrect the same person, giving him or her a newly formed body.

15. (a) What does the term "resurrection" mean? (b) Why will the resurrection of individuals pose no problem for Jehovah God?

Just as Jesus called Lazarus from the tomb, so millions will be resurrected

Joy will prevail when 'God swallows up death forever'

¹⁶ Jesus Christ said: "The hour is coming in which all those in the memorial tombs will hear his [Jesus'] voice and come out, those who did good things to a resurrection of life, those who practiced vile things to a resurrection of judgment." (John 5:28, 29) All those in Jehovah's memory will be resurrected and instructed in his ways. For those who act in harmony with the knowledge of God, this will turn out to be a resurrection of life. However, it will turn out to be a resurrection of condemnatory judgment for those who reject God's teachings and rulership.

¹⁷ Naturally, those who have pursued a righteous course as Jehovah's servants will be resurrected. In fact, the resurrection hope strengthened many to face death, even in cases of violent persecution. They knew that God could restore them to life. (Matthew 10:28) But millions of people have died without showing whether they would comply with God's righteous standards. They too will be resurrected. Confident in Jehovah's purpose in this regard, the apostle Paul said: "I have hope toward God . . . that there is going to be a resurrection of both the righteous and the unrighteous."—Acts 24:15.

¹⁸ The apostle John received a thrilling vision of resurrected ones standing before God's throne. John then wrote: "The sea gave up those dead in it, and death and Hades gave up those dead in them, and they were judged individually according to their deeds. And death and Hades were hurled into the lake of fire. This means

---

16. (a) What promise did Jesus make about all those in the memorial tombs? (b) What will determine how a person's resurrection turns out?

17. Who will be resurrected?

18. (a) The apostle John received what vision of the resurrection? (b) What is destroyed in "the lake of fire," and what does this "lake" symbolize?

the second death, the lake of fire." (Revelation 20:12-14) Think of that! All the dead who are in God's memory have the prospect of release from Hades (Greek, *hai'-des*), or Sheol, mankind's common grave. (Psalm 16:10; Acts 2:31) They will have an opportunity to demonstrate by their deeds whether they will serve God. Then "death and Hades" will be hurled into what is called "the lake of fire," symbolizing complete destruction, as does the term "Gehenna." (Luke 12:5) The common grave of mankind itself will have been emptied and will cease to exist when the resurrection is completed. How comforting it is to learn from the Bible that God does not torture anyone!—Jeremiah 7:30, 31.

RESURRECTION TO WHERE?

[19] A limited number of men and women will be resurrected to life in heaven. As kings and priests with Jesus, they will share in undoing all the effects of death that mankind inherited from the first man, Adam. (Romans 5:12; Revelation 5:9, 10) How many will God take to heaven to rule with Christ? According to the Bible, only 144,000. (Revelation 7:4; 14:1) Jehovah will give each of these resurrected ones a spirit body so that they can live in heaven.—1 Corinthians 15:35, 38, 42-45; 1 Peter 3:18.

[20] By far the majority of those who have died will be resurrected to a paradise earth. (Psalm 37:11, 29; Matthew 6:10) Part of the reason for resurrecting some to heaven is to complete God's purpose for the earth. Jesus Christ and the 144,000 in heaven will progressively bring obedient mankind back to the perfection that our original parents threw away. This will include resurrected ones, as indicated by Jesus when he told the dying

19. Why will some of mankind be resurrected to heaven, and what kind of body will God give them?
20. What will be experienced by obedient mankind, including resurrected ones?

man impaled next to him: "You will be with me in Paradise."—Luke 23:42, 43.

21 On the Paradise earth, death, which today produces such futility, will be removed. (Romans 8:19-21) The prophet Isaiah declared that Jehovah God "will actually swallow up death forever." (Isaiah 25:8) The apostle John was given a vision of the time when obedient mankind will experience freedom from pain and death. Yes, "God himself will be with them. And he will wipe out every tear from their eyes, and death will be no more, neither will mourning nor outcry nor pain be anymore. The former things have passed away."—Revelation 21:1-4.

22 The Bible's clear teachings remove confusion about what happens to the dead. The Scriptures plainly state that death is "the last enemy" that will be destroyed. (1 Corinthians 15:26) What strength and comfort we can draw from knowledge of the resurrection hope! And how glad we can be that our dead loved ones who are in God's memory will awaken from the sleep of death to enjoy all the good things he has in store for those who love him! (Psalm 145:16) Such blessings will be accomplished through God's Kingdom. But when was its rule to begin? Let us see.

---

21. According to the prophet Isaiah and the apostle John, what will happen to death?
22. How does knowledge of the resurrection affect you?

TEST YOUR KNOWLEDGE

What is the spirit in humans?
•
How would you describe the condition of the dead?
•
Who will be resurrected?

CHAPTER 10

GOD'S KINGDOM RULES

PERHAPS you have had the experience of buying a piece of equipment, only to find that it did not work. Let us say that you called a repairman. Shortly after he "fixed" the device, however, it broke down. How disappointing that was!

[2] It is similar with human governments. Mankind has always desired a government that would ensure peace and happiness. Yet, strenuous efforts to repair the breakdowns in society have not been truly successful. A great many peace treaties have been made—and then broken. Moreover, what government has been able to eradicate poverty, prejudice, crime, disease, and ecological ruin? Man's rule is beyond repair. Even Israel's wise King Solomon asked: "As regards earthling man, how can he discern his way?"—Proverbs 20:24.

[3] Do not despair! A stable world government is not just a dream. It was the theme of Jesus' preaching. He called it "the kingdom of God," and he taught his followers to pray for it. (Luke 11:2; 21:31) Of course, God's Kingdom is sometimes mentioned in religious circles. In fact, millions pray for it daily when they repeat the Lord's Prayer (also called the Our Father or model prayer). But people answer in various ways when asked, "What is God's Kingdom?" Some say, "It is in your heart." Others call it heaven. The Bible gives a clear answer, as we shall see.

1, 2. How have human governments proved inadequate?
3. (a) What was the theme of Jesus' preaching? (b) How do some people describe God's Kingdom?

A KINGDOM WITH A PURPOSE

[4] Jehovah God has always been King, or Sovereign Ruler, of the universe. The fact that he created all things elevates him to that exalted position. (1 Chronicles 29: 11; Psalm 103:19; Acts 4:24) But the Kingdom that Jesus preached about is subsidiary, or secondary, to God's universal sovereignty. That Messianic Kingdom has a specific purpose, but what is it?

[5] As explained in Chapter 6, the first human pair rebelled against God's authority. Because of the issues raised, Jehovah chose to bring about a new expression of his sovereignty. God announced his purpose to produce a "seed" that would crush the Serpent, Satan, and remove the effects of mankind's inherited sin. The primary "seed" is Jesus Christ, and "the kingdom of God" is the agency that will utterly defeat Satan. By means of this Kingdom, Jesus Christ will restore rulership over the earth in Jehovah's name and will vindicate God's rightful sovereignty for all time.—Genesis 3:15; Psalm 2:2-9.

[6] According to one rendition of Jesus' words to wicked Pharisees, he said: "The kingdom of God is within you." (Luke 17:21, *King James Version*) Did Jesus mean that the Kingdom was in the wicked hearts of those corrupt men? No. A more accurate translation of the original Greek reads: "The kingdom of God is *in your midst*." (*New World Translation*) Jesus, who was in their midst, thus referred to himself as the future King. Far from being something that a person has in his heart, God's Kingdom is a real, operating government having a ruler and subjects. It is a heavenly government, for it is called both "the kingdom of the heavens" and "the kingdom of God." (Matthew 13: 11; Luke 8:10) In vision, the prophet Daniel beheld its

---

4, 5. Why did Jehovah choose to bring about a new expression of his sovereignty, and what will it accomplish?

6, 7. (a) Where is the Kingdom, and who are the King and his associate rulers? (b) Who are the subjects of the Kingdom?

Ruler as "someone like a son of man" brought before Almighty God and given lasting "rulership and dignity and kingdom, that the peoples, national groups and languages should all serve even him." (Daniel 7:13, 14) Who is this King? Well, the Bible calls Jesus Christ "the Son of man." (Matthew 12:40; Luke 17:26) Yes, Jehovah designated his Son, Jesus Christ, to be King.

[7] Jesus does not rule alone. With him are 144,000 who have been "bought from the earth" to be his associate kings and priests. (Revelation 5:9, 10; 14:1, 3; Luke 22:28-30) The subjects of God's Kingdom will be a global family of humans who are submissive to Christ's leadership. (Psalm 72:7, 8) How, though, can we be sure that the Kingdom will actually vindicate God's sovereignty and restore paradisaic conditions to our earth?

THE REALITY OF GOD'S KINGDOM

[8] Imagine that a fire has destroyed your home. Now a friend who has the means to do so promises to help rebuild your house and provide food for your family. If that friend has always told you the truth, would you not believe him? Suppose you came home from work the next day and found that workers were already starting to clean up the debris from the fire and that food had been brought for your family. No doubt you would be completely confident that with the passing of time, things would not only be restored but would even be better than before.

[9] Similarly, Jehovah gives us assurance of the Kingdom's reality. As shown in the Bible book of Hebrews, many facets of the Law foreshadowed the Kingdom arrangement. (Hebrews 10:1) Foregleams of God's Kingdom were also evident in the earthly kingdom of Israel. That was no ordinary government, for the rulers sat upon

8, 9. (a) How might we illustrate the reliability of God's Kingdom promises? (b) Why can we be sure of the Kingdom's reality?

"Jehovah's throne." (1 Chronicles 29:23) Moreover, it had been foretold: "The scepter will not turn aside from Judah, neither the commander's staff from between his feet, until Shiloh comes; and to him the obedience of the peoples will belong." (Genesis 49:10)* Yes, it was into this Judean line of kings that Jesus, the permanent King of God's government, was to be born.—Luke 1:32, 33.

¹⁰ The foundation of God's Messianic Kingdom was laid with the selection of Jesus' apostles. (Ephesians 2: 19, 20; Revelation 21:14) These were the first of 144,000 who would rule in heaven as associate kings with Jesus Christ. While on earth, these prospective corulers would spearhead a witnessing campaign, in keeping with Jesus' command: "Go . . . and make disciples of people of all the nations, baptizing them in the name of the Father and of the Son and of the holy spirit."—Matthew 28:19.

¹¹ The command to make disciples is now being obeyed on an unprecedented scale. Jehovah's Witnesses are proclaiming the good news of the Kingdom all around the globe, in harmony with Jesus' prophetic words: "This good news of the kingdom will be preached in all the inhabited earth for a witness to all the nations; and then the end will come." (Matthew 24:14) As one aspect of the Kingdom-preaching work, a great educational program is being carried out. Those who submit to the laws and principles of God's Kingdom are already experiencing a peace

---

* The name Shiloh means "He Whose It Is; He to Whom It Belongs." In time, it became evident that "Shiloh" was Jesus Christ, "the Lion that is of the tribe of Judah." (Revelation 5:5) Some of the Jewish Targums simply replaced the word "Shiloh" with "the Messiah" or "the king Messiah."

10. (a) When was the foundation of God's Messianic Kingdom laid? (b) What important work would Jesus' prospective corulers be spearheading on earth?
11. How is the Kingdom-preaching work being carried out today, and what is it accomplishing?

SOME IMPORTANT EVENTS RELATED TO GOD'S KINGDOM

• Jehovah announces his purpose to produce a "seed" that would crush the head of the Serpent, Satan the Devil.—Genesis 3:15.

• In 1943 B.C.E., Jehovah indicates that this "seed" would be a human descendant of Abraham.—Genesis 12:1-3, 7; 22:18.

• The Law covenant given to Israel in 1513 B.C.E. provides "a shadow of the good things to come."—Exodus 24:6-8; Hebrews 10:1.

• The earthly kingdom of Israel commences in 1117 B.C.E., and it continues later in the line of David.—1 Samuel 11:15; 2 Samuel 7:8, 16.

• Jerusalem is destroyed in 607 B.C.E., and "the appointed times of the nations" begin.—2 Kings 25:8-10, 25, 26; Luke 21:24.

• In 29 C.E., Jesus is anointed as King-Designate and proceeds with his earthly ministry.—Matthew 3:16, 17; 4:17; 21:9-11.

• In 33 C.E., Jesus ascends to heaven, there to wait at God's right hand until his rule begins.—Acts 5:30, 31; Hebrews 10:12, 13.

• Jesus is enthroned in the heavenly Kingdom in 1914 C.E. as "the appointed times of the nations" end.—Revelation 11:15.

• Satan and his demons are cast down to the vicinity of the earth and bring increased woe to mankind.—Revelation 12:9-12.

• Jesus oversees the worldwide preaching of the good news of God's Kingdom.—Matthew 24:14; 28:19, 20.

and unity that human governments cannot achieve. All of this gives clear evidence that God's Kingdom is a reality!

¹² Jehovah told the Israelites: "You are my witnesses, . . . even my servant whom I have chosen." (Isaiah 43:10-12) Jesus, "the Faithful Witness," zealously declared the good news of the Kingdom. (Revelation 1:5; Matthew 4:17) So it is appropriate that present-day Kingdom proclaimers bear the divinely appointed name Jehovah's Witness-

---

12. (a) Why is it appropriate to call Kingdom proclaimers Jehovah's Witnesses? (b) How does God's Kingdom differ from human governments?

es. But why do the Witnesses spend so much time and effort talking to others about God's Kingdom? They do this because the Kingdom is mankind's only hope. Human governments break down sooner or later, but God's Kingdom never will. Isaiah 9:6, 7 calls its Ruler, Jesus, the "Prince of Peace" and adds: "To the abundance of the princely rule and to peace there will be no end." God's Kingdom is not like man's governments—here today and overthrown tomorrow. Indeed, Daniel 2:44 says: "The God of heaven will set up a kingdom that will never be brought to ruin. And the kingdom itself will not be passed on to any other people.... It itself will stand to times indefinite."

¹³ What human king could bring about the elimination of war, crime, sickness, starvation, and homelessness? Furthermore, what earthly ruler could resurrect those who have died? God's Kingdom and its King will address these matters. The Kingdom will not prove defective, like malfunctioning equipment that continually needs repair. Rather, God's Kingdom will succeed, for Jehovah promises: "My word that goes forth from my mouth ... will not return to me without results, but it will certainly do that in which I have delighted, and it will have certain success in that for which I have sent it." (Isaiah 55:11) God's purpose will not fail, but when was Kingdom rule to begin?

KINGDOM RULE—WHEN?

¹⁴ "Lord, are you restoring the kingdom to Israel at this time?" This question posed by Jesus' disciples revealed that as yet they did not know the purpose of God's Kingdom and the appointed time for its rule to begin.

13. (a) What are some problems that God's Kingdom will address successfully? (b) Why can we be sure that God's promises will be fulfilled?
14. What misunderstanding did Jesus' disciples have regarding the Kingdom, but what did Jesus know about his rulership?

Warning them not to speculate about the matter, Jesus said: "It does not belong to you to get knowledge of the times or seasons which the Father has placed in his own jurisdiction." Jesus knew that his rulership over the earth was reserved for the future, long after his resurrection and ascension to heaven. (Acts 1:6-11; Luke 19:11, 12, 15) The Scriptures had foretold this. How so?

¹⁵ Prophetically referring to Jesus as "Lord," King David said: "The utterance of Jehovah to my Lord is: 'Sit at my right hand until I place your enemies as a stool for your feet.'" (Psalm 110:1; compare Acts 2:34-36.) This prophecy indicates that Jesus' rulership would not begin immediately after his ascension to heaven. Rather, he would wait at God's right hand. (Hebrews 10:12, 13) How long would this waiting go on? When would his rulership begin? The Bible helps us to find the answers.

¹⁶ The only city in all the earth upon which Jehovah placed his name was Jerusalem. (1 Kings 11:36) It was also the capital of a God-approved earthly kingdom typical of God's heavenly Kingdom. Therefore, the destruction of Jerusalem by the Babylonians in 607 B.C.E. was very significant. This event marked the beginning of a lengthy interruption of God's direct rule over his people on earth. Some six centuries later, Jesus indicated that this period of interrupted rule was still in effect, for he said: "Jerusalem will be trampled on by the nations, until the appointed times of the nations are fulfilled."—Luke 21:24.

¹⁷ During "the appointed times of the nations," worldly governments would be allowed to interrupt rulership ap-

15. How does Psalm 110:1 shed light on the timing of Jesus' rulership?
16. What happened in 607 B.C.E., and how was this related to God's Kingdom?
17. (a) What are "the appointed times of the nations," and how long were they to last? (b) When did "the appointed times of the nations" begin and end?

proved by God. That period began with the destruction
of Jerusalem in 607 B.C.E., and Daniel indicated that it
would go on for "seven times." (Daniel 4:23-25) How long
is that? The Bible shows that three and a half "times"
equal 1,260 days. (Revelation 12:6, 14) Twice that period,
or seven times, would be 2,520 days. But nothing note-
worthy happened at the end of that short period of time.
By applying "a day for a year" to Daniel's prophecy and
counting 2,520 years from 607 B.C.E., however, we arrive
at the year 1914 C.E.—Numbers 14:34; Ezekiel 4:6.

[18] Did Jesus begin to reign in heaven at that time? Scriptural reasons for saying that he did will be discussed in
the next chapter. Of course, the beginning of Jesus' rule
would not be marked by immediate peace on the earth.
Revelation 12:7-12 shows that just after receiving the
Kingdom, Jesus would oust Satan and the demon angels
from heaven. This would mean woe for the earth, but it is
heartening to read that the Devil has only "a short period
of time" left. Soon, we will be able to rejoice not only because God's Kingdom rules but also because it will bring
blessings to the earth and obedient mankind. (Psalm 72:
7, 8) How do we know that this will happen soon?

---

18. What did Jesus do shortly after receiving Kingdom power, and
how did this affect the earth?

TEST YOUR KNOWLEDGE

What is God's Kingdom, and from where does it rule?
•
Who rules in the Kingdom, and who are its subjects?
•
How has Jehovah assured us that his
Kingdom is a reality?
•
When did "the appointed times of the
nations" begin and end?

CHAPTER 11

THESE ARE
THE LAST DAYS!

HOW did our turbulent world get to this point? Where are we heading? Have you ever asked such questions? Many feel somewhat lost when they look at the world scene. Realities such as warfare, disease, and crime leave people wondering what the future holds. Government leaders offer little hope. However, a reliable explanation of these distressing days is available from God in his Word. The Bible reliably helps us to see where we are in the stream of time. It shows us that we are in "the last days" of the present system of things.—2 Timothy 3:1.

² Consider, for example, the answer Jesus gave to some questions raised by his disciples. Three days before Jesus died, they asked him: "What will be the sign of your presence and of the conclusion of the system of things?"* (Matthew 24:3) In reply, Jesus told of specific world events and

---

* Some Bibles use the word "world" instead of "system of things." W. E. Vine's *Expository Dictionary of New Testament Words* says that the Greek word *ai·on′* "signifies a period of indefinite duration, or time viewed in relation to what takes place in the period." Parkhurst's *Greek and English Lexicon to the New Testament* (page 17) includes the expression "this system of things" in discussing the use of *ai·o′nes* (plural) at Hebrews 1:2. So the rendering "system of things" is in harmony with the original Greek text.

1. Why do many feel somewhat lost when contemplating the world scene, but where can a reliable explanation of world events be found?
2. What question was Jesus asked by his disciples, and how did he reply?

situations that would clearly show that this ungodly system had entered its last days.

[3] As shown in the preceding chapter, Bible chronology leads to the conclusion that God's Kingdom has already begun to rule. But how can that be? Things have become worse, not better. Actually, this is a strong indication that God's Kingdom *has* begun ruling. Why so? Well, Psalm 110:2 informs us that for a time Jesus would rule 'in the midst of his enemies.' Indeed, his first act as heavenly King was to cast Satan and his demon angels down to the vicinity of the earth. (Revelation 12:9) What was the effect? It was just what Revelation 12:12 foretold: "Woe for the earth and for the sea, because the Devil has come down to you, having great anger, knowing he has a short period of time." We are now living in that "short period of time."

[4] Not surprisingly, therefore, when Jesus was asked what the sign of his presence and of the conclusion of the system of things would be, his reply was sobering. Various components of the sign are found in the box on page 102. As you can see, the Christian apostles Paul, Peter, and John provide us with further details concerning the last days. True, most features of the sign and of the last days involve distressing situations. Yet, the fulfillment of these prophecies should convince us that this wicked system is near its end. Let us take a close look at some of the principal features of the last days.

FEATURES OF THE LAST DAYS

[5] *"Nation will rise against nation and kingdom against kingdom."* (Matthew 24:7; Revelation 6:4) Writer Ernest

---

3. Why did conditions on earth get worse when Jesus began to rule?
4. What are some features of the last days, and what do they indicate? (See box.)
5, 6. How are prophecies regarding warfare and famine being fulfilled?

Hemingway called World War I "the most colossal, murderous, mismanaged butchery that has ever taken place on earth." According to the book *The World in the Crucible—1914-1919,* this was "a new scope of war, the first total war in the experience of mankind. Its duration, intensity, and scale exceeded anything previously known or generally expected." Then came World War II, which proved much more destructive than World War I. "The twentieth century," says professor of history Hugh Thomas, "has been dominated by the machine gun, the tank, the B-52, the nuclear bomb and, finally, the missile. It has been marked by wars more bloody and destructive than those of any other age." True, much was said about disarmament after the Cold War ended. Still, one report estimates

SOME FEATURES OF THE LAST DAYS

- Unprecedented warfare.—Matthew 24:7; Revelation 6:4.
- Famine.—Matthew 24:7; Revelation 6:5, 6, 8.
- Pestilences.—Luke 21:11; Revelation 6:8.
- Increasing lawlessness.—Matthew 24:12.
- Ruining of the earth.—Revelation 11:18.
- Earthquakes.—Matthew 24:7.
- Critical times hard to deal with.—2 Timothy 3:1.
- Inordinate love of money.—2 Timothy 3:2.
- Disobedience to parents.—2 Timothy 3:2.
- A lack of natural affection.—2 Timothy 3:3.
- Loving pleasures rather than God.—2 Timothy 3:4.
- A lack of self-control.—2 Timothy 3:3.
- Without love of goodness.—2 Timothy 3:3.
- Taking no note of the impending danger.—Matthew 24:39.
- Ridiculers reject proof of the last days.—2 Peter 3:3, 4.
- Global preaching of God's Kingdom.—Matthew 24:14.

that after proposed reductions some 10,000 to 20,000 nuclear warheads will remain—more than 900 times the firepower used during World War II.

[6] *"There will be food shortages."* (Matthew 24:7; Revelation 6:5, 6, 8) Since 1914 there have been at least 20 major famines. Afflicted areas include Bangladesh, Burundi, Cambodia, China, Ethiopia, Greece, India, Nigeria, Russia, Rwanda, Somalia, and Sudan. But famine is not always caused by a lack of food. "The world's food supply over recent decades has grown faster than its population," concluded a group of agricultural scientists and economists. "But because at least 800 million people remain in deep poverty, . . . they are unable to purchase enough of the abundance to lift them out of chronic malnutrition." Political meddling is involved in other cases. Dr. Abdelgalil Elmekki of the University of Toronto cites two examples in which thousands starved while their countries were exporting massive amounts of food.

The governments seemed far more concerned with raising foreign currency to finance their wars than with feeding their citizens. Dr. Elmekki's conclusion? Famine is often "a matter of distribution and government policy."

[7] *"Pestilences."* (Luke 21:11; Revelation 6:8) The Spanish influenza of 1918-19 claimed at least 21 million lives. "The world had never in history been ravaged by a killer that slew so many human beings so quickly," writes A. A. Hoehling in *The Great Epidemic.* Today, pestilences rage on. Each year, cancer kills five million people, diarrheal diseases claim the lives of more than three million infants and children, and tuberculosis slays three million. Respiratory infections, mainly pneumonia, annually kill 3.5 million youngsters under five years of age. And a staggering 2.5 billion—half the world's population—suffer from sicknesses that stem from insufficient or contaminated water and poor sanitation. AIDS looms as a further reminder that man, despite his significant medical accomplishments, is incapable of eradicating pestilences.

[8] *"Men will be . . . lovers of money."* (2 Timothy 3:2) In lands around the world, people seem to have an insatiable hunger for greater wealth. "Success" is often measured by the size of one's paycheck, "accomplishment" by how much one owns. "Materialism will continue to be one of the driving forces in American society . . . and an increasingly important force in other major markets as well," declared the vice president of an advertising agency. Is this happening where you live?

[9] *"Disobedient to parents."* (2 Timothy 3:2) Present-day parents, teachers, and others have firsthand evidence that many children are disrespectful and disobedient. Some of these youngsters are either reacting to or imitating their parents' misbehavior. Increasing numbers of children are

---

7. What are the facts about pestilences today?
8. How are people proving to be "lovers of money"?
9. What can be said about the foretold disobedience to parents?

losing faith in—and rebelling against—school, the law, religion, and their parents. "As a trend," says one veteran schoolteacher, "they seem to have very little respect for anything." Happily, though, many God-fearing children are exemplary in behavior.

[10] *"Fierce."* (2 Timothy 3:3) The Greek word translated "fierce" means 'untamed, wild, lacking human sympathy and feeling.' How well this fits many perpetrators of today's violence! "Life is so traumatic, so bloodied with horror that it takes a cast-iron stomach to read the daily news," said one editorial. A housing-police sergeant noted that many youths seem to blind themselves to the consequences of their actions. He said: "There is a feeling that, 'I don't know about tomorrow. I'll get what I want today.'"

[11] *"Having no natural affection."* (2 Timothy 3:3) This phrase is translated from a Greek word meaning "heartless, inhuman" and denoting a "lack of natural, family affection." (*The New International Dictionary of New Testament Theology*) Yes, affection is often missing in the very environment in which it should flourish—the home. Reports of abusive treatment of marriage mates, children, and even of elderly parents have become disturbingly common. One research team commented: "Human violence—be it a slap or a shove, a knifing or a shoot-out—occurs more frequently within the family circle than anywhere else in our society."

[12] *"Having a form of godly devotion but proving false to its power."* (2 Timothy 3:5) The Bible has the power to change lives for the better. (Ephesians 4:22-24) Yet, many today use their religion as a screen behind which they carry on unrighteous activities that displease God. Lying, stealing, and sexual misconduct are often condoned by religious

---

10, 11. What evidence is there that people are fierce and lacking in natural affection?

12. Why can it be said that people have only a form of godly devotion?

leaders. Many religions preach love but support warfare. "In the name of the Supreme Creator," observes an editorial in the magazine *India Today,* "human beings have perpetrated the most abominable atrocities against their fellow creatures." In fact, the two bloodiest conflicts of recent times—World Wars I and II—erupted in the heart of Christendom.

¹³ *"Ruining the earth."* (Revelation 11:18) More than 1,600 scientists, including 104 Nobel laureates, from around the world endorsed a warning, issued by the Union of Concerned Scientists (UCS), that stated: "Human beings and the natural world are on a collision course. . . . No more than a few decades remain before the chance to avert the threats will be lost." The report said that man's life-threatening practices "may so alter the world that it will be unable to sustain life in the manner that we know." Ozone depletion, water pollution, deforestation, loss of soil productivity, and the extinction of many animal and plant species were cited as urgent problems that must be addressed. "Our tampering with the interdependent web of life," said the UCS, "could trigger widespread effects, including collapses of biological systems whose dynamics we imperfectly understand."

¹⁴ *"This good news of the kingdom will be preached in all the inhabited earth."* (Matthew 24:14) Jesus foretold that the good news of the Kingdom would be preached earth wide, for a witness to all the nations. With divine help and blessing, millions of Jehovah's Witnesses are devoting billions of hours to this preaching and disciple-making work. (Matthew 28:19, 20) Yes, the Witnesses realize that they would be bloodguilty if they did not declare the good news. (Ezekiel 3:18, 19) But they are delighted that each year thousands gratefully respond to the Kingdom

---

13. What evidence is there that the earth is being ruined?
14. How could you prove that Matthew 24:14 is being fulfilled in our day?

message and take their stand as true Christians, that is, as Witnesses of Jehovah. It is an inestimable privilege to serve Jehovah and thus spread the knowledge of God. And after this good news is preached in all the inhabited earth, the end of this wicked system will come.

RESPOND TO THE EVIDENCE

[15] How will this system end? The Bible foretells a "great tribulation" that will begin with an attack by this world's political element upon "Babylon the Great," the world empire of false religion. (Matthew 24:21; Revelation 17:5, 16) Jesus said that during this period 'the sun would be darkened, and the moon would not give its light, and the stars would fall from heaven, and the powers of the heavens would be shaken.' (Matthew 24:29) This may denote literal celestial phenomena. In any case, the shining lights of the religious world will be exposed and eliminated. Then Satan, called "Gog of the land of Magog," will use corrupted humans in making an all-out assault upon Jehovah's people. But Satan will not succeed, for God will come to their rescue. (Ezekiel 38:1, 2, 14-23) "The great tribulation" will reach its climax in Armageddon, "the war of the great day of God the Almighty." It will clean out every last vestige of Satan's earthly organization, opening the way for endless blessings to flow to surviving mankind.—Revelation 7:9, 14; 11:15; 16:14, 16; 21:3, 4.

[16] By themselves, some features of the prophecies describing the last days might seem to apply to other periods of history. But when combined, the prophesied evidences pinpoint our day. To illustrate: The lines making up a person's fingerprint form a pattern that cannot belong to any other individual. Similarly, the last days have their own pattern of marks, or happenings. These form a "finger-

---

15. How will the present wicked system end?
16. How do we know that the prophesied features of the last days apply to our time?

print" that cannot belong to any other time period. When considered along with Bible indications that God's heavenly Kingdom is now ruling, the evidence provides a solid basis for concluding that these are indeed the last days. Moreover, there is clear Scriptural proof that the present wicked system will soon be destroyed.

¹⁷ How will you respond to the evidence that these are the last days? Consider this: If a fiercely destructive storm is impending, we take precautionary measures without delay. Well, what the Bible foretells for this present system should move us to action. (Matthew 16:1-3) We can clearly see that we are living in the last days of this world system. This should motivate us to make any adjustments necessary to gain God's favor. (2 Peter 3:3, 10-12) Referring to himself as the agent for salvation, Jesus sounds the urgent call: "Pay attention to yourselves that your hearts never become weighed down with overeating and heavy drinking and anxieties of life, and suddenly that day be instantly upon you as a snare. For it will come in upon all those dwelling upon the face of all the earth. Keep awake, then, all the time making supplication that you may succeed in escaping all these things that are destined to occur, and in standing before the Son of man." —Luke 21:34-36.

17. What should the knowledge that these are the last days move us to do?

TEST YOUR KNOWLEDGE

What did the Bible foretell about world developments at the onset of Christ's rule?

•

What are some features of the last days?

•

What convinces you that these are the last days?

CHAPTER 12

RESIST WICKED SPIRIT FORCES

RIGHT after his baptism, Jesus Christ went into the Judean wilderness to pray and meditate. There Satan the Devil tried to get him to break God's law. However, Jesus rejected the Devil's bait and did not get caught in his trap. Jesus faced other wicked spirits during his ministry on earth. Yet, time and again, he rebuked and resisted them.—Luke 4:1-13; 8:26-34; 9:37-43.

² Bible accounts describing those encounters should convince us that wicked spirit forces do exist. They try to mislead people. However, we can resist these evil spirits. But where do wicked spirits come from? Why do they try to deceive humans? And what methods do they use to achieve their ends? Finding the answers to such questions as these will help you to resist wicked spirit forces.

WICKED SPIRITS
—THEIR ORIGIN AND TARGET

³ Jehovah God made a multitude of spirit creatures long before he created humans. (Job 38:4, 7) As explained in Chapter 6, one of these angels developed a desire to have humans worship him instead of worshiping Jehovah. Pursuing that objective, this wicked angel re-

---

1. How did Jesus react when he encountered wicked spirits?
2. We will consider what questions?
3. How did Satan the Devil come to be?

sisted and slandered the Creator, even suggesting to the first woman that God was a liar. Fittingly, then, this rebellious spirit creature became known as Satan (resister) the Devil (slanderer).—Genesis 3:1-5; Job 1:6.

⁴ Later, other angels sided with Satan the Devil. In the days of the righteous man Noah, some of these abandoned their service in heaven and took on fleshly bodies to satisfy their lust for sexual relations with earthly women. Satan no doubt influenced those angels to take that disobedient course. It led to their fathering the hybrid offspring called Nephilim, who became violent bullies. When Jehovah caused the great Deluge, it destroyed corrupted mankind and this unnatural progeny of the disobedient angels. The rebellious angels escaped destruction by dematerializing their fleshly bodies and returning to the spirit realm. But God restrained these demons by treating them as outcasts in spiritual darkness. (Genesis 6:1-7, 17; Jude 6) Satan, "the ruler of the demons," and his wicked angels nevertheless have pushed on with their rebellion. (Luke 11:15) What is their goal?

⁵ The evil objective of Satan and the demons is to turn people against Jehovah God. Hence, these wicked ones have been misleading, frightening, and assaulting people throughout human history. (Revelation 12:9) Modern-day examples confirm that demon aggression is more vicious now than it has ever been. To entrap people, the demons often use spiritism in all its forms. How do the demons use this bait, and how can you defend yourself?

---

4. How did certain angels sin in Noah's day?

5. Satan and his demons have what objective, and what do they use to entrap people?

How do you view spiritism in its many forms?

HOW WICKED SPIRITS
TRY TO MISLEAD YOU

6 What is spiritism? It is involvement with demons, or wicked spirits, either directly or through a human medium. Spiritism does for demons what bait does for hunters: It attracts prey. And just as a hunter uses a variety of baits to lure animals into his trap, so wicked spirits encourage various forms of spiritism to bring humans under their control. (Compare Psalm 119:110.) Some of these forms are divination, magic, looking for omens, sorcery, binding with spells, consulting mediums, and inquiring of the dead.

7 The bait works, for spiritism attracts people around the world. Those living in jungle villages go to medicine men, and city office workers consult astrologers. Spiritism flourishes even in so-called Christian lands. Research indicates that in the United States alone, some 30 magazines with a combined circulation of over 10,000,-000 are devoted to various forms of spiritism. Brazilians spend over 500 million dollars on spiritistic items each year. Yet, 80 percent of those frequenting spiritistic centers of worship in that country are baptized Catholics who also attend Mass. Inasmuch as some clergymen practice spiritism, many religious people think that practicing it is acceptable to God. But is it?

WHY THE BIBLE CONDEMNS
THE PRACTICE OF SPIRITISM

8 If you have been taught that some forms of spiritism are means of contacting good spirits, you may be surprised to learn what the Bible says about spiritism.

---

6. What is spiritism, and what are some forms of it?
7. How widespread is spiritism, and why does it flourish even in so-called Christian lands?
8. What is the Scriptural view of spiritism?

Jehovah's people were warned: "Do not turn yourselves to the spirit mediums, and do not consult professional foretellers of events, so as to become *unclean* by them." (Leviticus 19:31; 20:6, 27) The Bible book of Revelation gives the warning that "those practicing spiritism" will end up in "the lake that burns with fire and sulphur. This means the second [everlasting] death." (Revelation 21:8; 22:15) All forms of spiritism are disapproved by Jehovah God. (Deuteronomy 18:10-12) Why is that the case?

⁹ Jehovah sent good spirits, or righteous angels, to communicate with some humans before the Bible was completed. Since its completion, God's Word has provided the guidance humans need to serve Jehovah acceptably. (2 Timothy 3:16, 17; Hebrews 1:1, 2) He does not bypass his holy Word by giving messages to mediums. All such present-day messages from the spirit world come from wicked spirits. The practice of spiritism can lead to demon harassment or even possession by wicked spirits. Therefore, God lovingly warns us not to get involved in any spiritistic practices. (Deuteronomy 18:14; Galatians 5:19-21) Moreover, if we continued to practice spiritism after knowing Jehovah's view of it, we would be siding with the rebellious wicked spirits and would be enemies of God.—1 Samuel 15:23; 1 Chronicles 10:13, 14; Psalm 5:4.

¹⁰ One popular form of spiritism is divination—attempting to find out about the future or the unknown with the help of spirits. Some forms of divination are astrology, crystal-ball gazing, interpretation of dreams, palmistry, and fortune-telling with the use of tarot cards.

9. Why can we conclude that present-day messages from the spirit world are not from Jehovah?
10. What is divination, and why should we avoid it?

Many view divination as harmless fun, but the Bible shows that fortune-tellers and wicked spirits go hand in hand. For example, Acts 16:16-19 mentions "a demon of divination" that enabled a certain girl to practice "the art of prediction." However, her ability to foretell the future was lost when the demon was expelled. Clearly, divination is a bait used by the demons to lure people into their trap.

¹¹ If you are grieving over the death of a beloved family member or a close friend, you could easily be enticed by another bait. A spirit medium may give you special information or may speak in a voice that seems to be that of the dead person. Beware! Attempts to communicate with the dead lead into a trap. Why? Because the dead cannot speak. As you no doubt recall, God's Word plainly says that at death a person "goes back to his ground; in that day his thoughts do perish." The dead "are conscious of nothing at all." (Psalm 146:4; Ecclesiastes 9:5, 10) Moreover, it is actually the demons who have been known to imitate the voice of the deceased and give a spirit medium information about the one who has died. (1 Samuel 28:3-19) So "anyone who inquires of the dead" is being entrapped by wicked spirits and is acting contrary to the will of Jehovah God.—Deuteronomy 18:11, 12; Isaiah 8:19.

FROM ATTRACTING TO ATTACKING

¹² When you comply with the counsel of God's Word regarding spiritism, you spurn the bait of the demons. (Compare Psalm 141:9, 10; Romans 12:9.) Does this

11. How do attempts to communicate with the dead lead into a trap?

12, 13. What evidence is there that the demons persist in tempting and harassing people?

mean that wicked spirits will stop trying to capture you? By no means! After tempting Jesus three times, Satan "retired from him until another convenient time." (Luke 4:13) Similarly, obstinate spirits not only attract people but also attack them.

¹³ Recall our earlier consideration of Satan's attack on God's servant Job. The Devil caused the loss of his livestock and the death of most of his servants. Satan even killed Job's children. Next, he struck Job himself with a painful disease. But Job kept his integrity to God and was greatly blessed. (Job 1:7-19; 2:7, 8; 42:12) Since then, the demons have made some people speechless or blind and have continued to revel in the suffering of humans. (Matthew 9:32, 33; 12:22; Mark 5:2-5) Today, reports show that demons sexually harass some and drive others to insanity. They incite still others to murder and suicide, which are sins against God. (Deuteronomy 5:17; 1 John 3:15) Nonetheless, thousands of people once ensnared by these wicked spirits have been able to break free. How has this been possible for them? They have done so by taking vital steps.

HOW TO RESIST WICKED SPIRITS

¹⁴ What is one way that you can resist wicked spirits and protect yourself and your family from their snares? First-century Christians in Ephesus who had practiced spiritism before becoming believers took positive steps. We read that "quite a number of those who practiced magical arts brought their books together and burned them up before everybody." (Acts 19:19) Even if you have not practiced spiritism, get rid of anything having spiritistic uses or overtones. This includes books, mag-

14. In harmony with the example of first-century Ephesian Christians, how can you resist wicked spirits?

azines, videos, posters, musical recordings, and objects used for spiritistic purposes. Also included are idols, amulets and other items worn for protection, and gifts received from practicers of spiritism. (Deuteronomy 7: 25, 26; 1 Corinthians 10:21) To illustrate: A married couple in Thailand had long been harassed by demons. Then they got rid of objects associated with spiritism. What was the result? They were relieved of the demonic attacks and thereafter made real spiritual progress.

¹⁵ In order to resist wicked spirits, another necessary step is to apply the apostle Paul's counsel to put on the complete suit of God-given spiritual armor. (Ephesians 6:11-17) Christians must fortify their defenses against wicked spirits. What does this step include? "Above all things," said Paul, "take up the large shield of faith, with which you will be able to quench all the wicked one's burning missiles." Indeed, the stronger your faith, the greater will be your ability to resist wicked spirit forces. —Matthew 17:14-20.

¹⁶ How can you strengthen your faith? By continuing to study the Bible and apply its counsel in your life. The strength of one's faith depends largely on the firmness of its base—the knowledge of God. Do you not agree that the accurate knowledge you have gained and taken to heart as you have studied the Bible has built up your faith? (Romans 10:10, 17) No doubt, therefore, as you continue this study and make it your custom to attend the meetings of Jehovah's Witnesses, your faith will be fortified even more. (Romans 1:11, 12; Colossians 2: 6, 7) It will be a mighty bulwark against demon attacks. —1 John 5:5.

15. In resisting wicked spirit forces, what is another necessary step?

16. How can you strengthen your faith?

¹⁷ What further steps might be taken by a person who is determined to resist wicked spirit forces? Ephesian Christians needed protection because they lived in a city infested with demonism. Hence, Paul told them: "Carry on prayer on every occasion in spirit." (Ephesians 6:18) Since we live in a demon-infested world, praying intensely for God's protection is essential in resisting wicked spirits. (Matthew 6:13) Helpful in this regard is the spiritual assistance and prayers of appointed elders in the Christian congregation.—James 5:13-15.

KEEP UP YOUR FIGHT AGAINST WICKED SPIRITS

¹⁸ Even after taking these basic steps, however, some have been troubled by wicked spirits. For instance, one man in Côte d'Ivoire studied the Bible with Jehovah's Witnesses and destroyed all his amulets. Thereafter, he made fine progress, dedicated his life to Jehovah, and was baptized. But a week after his baptism, the demons began to trouble him again, and voices told him to abandon his newfound faith. If this happened to you, would it mean that you had lost Jehovah's protection? Not necessarily.

¹⁹ Though the perfect man Jesus Christ had divine protection, he heard the voice of the wicked spirit creature Satan the Devil. Jesus showed what to do in such a case. He told the Devil: "Go away, Satan!" (Matthew 4: 3-10) In like manner, you should refuse to listen to voices from the spirit world. Resist wicked spirits by calling on Jehovah for help. Yes, pray aloud using God's name. Proverbs 18:10 says: "The name of Jehovah is a strong

---

17. What further steps may be necessary in resisting wicked spirit forces?
18, 19. What can be done if the demons again trouble a person?

tower. Into it the righteous runs and is given protection." The Christian man in Côte d'Ivoire did this, and the wicked spirits stopped harassing him.—Psalm 124:8; 145:18.

[20] Jehovah has allowed the wicked spirits to remain in existence, but he shows his power, particularly in behalf of his people, and his name is being declared in all the earth. (Exodus 9:16) If you stay close to God, you need not fear wicked spirits. (Numbers 23:21, 23; James 4:7, 8; 2 Peter 2:9) Their power is limited. They were punished in Noah's day, were cast out of heaven in recent times, and are now awaiting final judgment. (Jude 6; Revelation 12:9; 20:1-3, 7-10, 14) In fact, they dread their coming destruction. (James 2:19) So whether wicked spirits try to attract you with some kind of bait or attack you in any way, you can resist them. (2 Corinthians 2:11) Shun every form of spiritism, apply the counsel of God's Word, and seek Jehovah's approval. Do this without delay, for your life depends on your resisting wicked spirit forces!

20. In summary, what can you do to resist wicked spirits?

TEST YOUR KNOWLEDGE

How do wicked spirits try
to mislead people?

Why does the
Bible condemn spiritism?

How can a person break free from
wicked spirit forces?

Why should you keep resisting
wicked spirits?

CHAPTER 13

WHY LIVING A GODLY LIFE BRINGS HAPPINESS

JEHOVAH is "the happy God," and he wants you to enjoy life. (1 Timothy 1:11) By walking in his way, you can benefit yourself and experience tranquillity that is deep and lasting, like an ever-flowing river. Walking in God's way also moves one to perform continuous acts of righteousness, "like the waves of the sea." This brings true happiness.—Isaiah 48:17, 18.

2 Some may object, 'People sometimes suffer for doing what is right.' True, and that is what happened to Jesus' apostles. Although persecuted, however, they rejoiced and went on "declaring the good news about the Christ." (Acts 5:40-42) We can learn important lessons from this. One is that our living a godly life does not guarantee that we will always be treated well. "In fact," wrote the apostle Paul, "all those desiring to live with godly devotion in association with Christ Jesus will also be persecuted." (2 Timothy 3:12) The reason for this is that Satan and his world are opposed to those who live in a godly way. (John 15:18, 19; 1 Peter 5:8) But genuine happiness is not dependent on external things. Rather, it comes from a conviction that we are doing what is right and therefore have God's smile of approval.—Matthew 5:10-12; James 1:2, 3; 1 Peter 4:13, 14.

---

1. Why can we say that Jehovah's way brings happiness?
2. How can Christians be happy though they are sometimes treated badly?

³ There are people who feel that they can earn God's favor through occasional acts of devotion but can forget about him at other times. True worship of Jehovah God is not like that. It affects a person's conduct throughout all his waking hours, from day to day, year after year. That is why it is also called "The Way." (Acts 19:9; Isaiah 30:21) It is a godly way of living that calls upon us to speak and act in harmony with God's Word.

⁴ When new students of the Bible see that they need to make some changes in order to please Jehovah, they may wonder, 'Is a godly life really worth living?' You can be sure that it is. Why? Because "God is love," and his ways are therefore meant to benefit us. (1 John 4:8) God is also wise and knows what is best for us. Since Jehovah God is almighty, he is able to strengthen us to fulfill our desire to please him by breaking a bad habit. (Philippians 4:13) Let us consider some principles involved in godly living and see how applying them brings happiness.

HONESTY RESULTS IN HAPPINESS

⁵ Jehovah is "the God of truth." (Psalm 31:5) No doubt, you desire to follow his example and be known as a truthful person. Honesty leads to self-respect and a feeling of well-being. Because dishonesty is so common in this sinful world, however, Christians need this reminder: "Speak truth each one of you with his neighbor . . . Let the stealer steal no more, but rather let him do hard work . . . that he may have something to distribute to someone in need." (Ephesians 4:25, 28) Christian employees do an honest day's work. Unless their employer gives permission, they do not take things that belong to him. Whether at work, in school, or at home, a worshiper of Jehovah must be

3. How should the worship of Jehovah affect a person's life?
4. Why is it beneficial to make changes so as to live according to God's ways?
5. What does the Bible say about lying and theft?

'honest in all things.' (Hebrews 13:18) Anyone who makes it a practice to lie or steal cannot have God's favor.—Deuteronomy 5:19; Revelation 21:8.

6 Being honest results in many blessings. Selina is a needy African widow who loves Jehovah God and his righteous principles. One day, she found a bag containing a bankbook and a large sum of money. Using a telephone directory, she was able to find the owner—a storekeeper who had been robbed. The man could not believe his eyes when Selina, though quite sick, visited him and returned the full contents of the bag. "Such honesty must be rewarded," he said and handed her a sum of money. More important, this man praised Selina's religion. Yes, honest deeds adorn Bible teaching, glorify Jehovah God, and bring happiness to his honest worshipers.—Titus 2:10; 1 Peter 2:12.

GENEROSITY BRINGS HAPPINESS

7 There is happiness in being generous, whereas greedy persons will not "inherit God's kingdom." (1 Corinthians 6:10) A common form of greed is gambling, which is an attempt to make money through the losses of others. Jehovah does not approve of those who are "greedy of dishonest gain." (1 Timothy 3:8) Even where gambling is legal and a person gambles for fun, he could become addicted and be promoting a practice that has ruined many lives. Gambling often brings hardship to the gambler's family, who may be left with little money to buy such necessities as food and clothing.—1 Timothy 6:10.

8 Because of their loving generosity, Christians find joy in assisting others, especially needy fellow believers. (James 2:15, 16) Before Jesus came to earth, he observed

---

6. How might a godly person's honesty bring glory to Jehovah?
7. What is wrong with gambling?
8. How did Jesus set a fine example of generosity, and how can we be generous?

God's generosity toward mankind. (Acts 14:16, 17) Jesus himself gave his time, his talents, and even his life in behalf of humankind. Hence, he was well qualified to say: "There is more happiness in giving than there is in receiving." (Acts 20:35) Jesus also spoke well of the poor widow who generously put two small coins in the temple treasure chest, for she gave "her whole living." (Mark 12:41-44) The ancient Israelites and the first-century Christians provide examples of joyful generosity in giving material support to the congregation and the Kingdom work. (1 Chronicles 29:9; 2 Corinthians 9:11-14) In addition to making material contributions for these purposes, present-day Christians happily offer praise to God and use their lives in his service. (Romans 12:1; Hebrews 13:15) Jehovah blesses them for using their time, energy, and other resources, including their funds, to support true worship and promote the worldwide work of preaching the good news of the Kingdom.—Proverbs 3:9, 10.

OTHER FACTORS PROMOTING HAPPINESS

9 To be happy, Christians must also 'guard their thinking abilities.' (Proverbs 5:1, 2) This requires that they read and meditate on God's Word and wholesome Bible literature. But there are things to avoid. For instance, excessive drinking of alcoholic beverages can make a person lose control of his thinking. In such a state, many people get involved in immoral behavior, act violently, and cause deadly accidents. No wonder the Bible says that drunkards will not inherit God's Kingdom! (1 Corinthians 6:10) Determined to stay "sound in mind," true Christians avoid drunkenness, and this helps to promote happiness among them.—Titus 2:2-6.

10 A clean body contributes to happiness. Yet, many

9. What is wrong with excessive drinking of alcoholic beverages?
10. (a) Why do Christians not use tobacco? (b) What benefits come from breaking addictive habits?

become addicted to harmful substances. For example, consider the use of tobacco. The World Health Organization reports that smoking "kills three million people each year." Breaking the tobacco habit can be difficult because of temporary withdrawal symptoms. On the other hand, many ex-smokers find that they have better health and more money for household needs. Yes, overcoming the tobacco habit or addiction to other harmful substances will contribute to a clean body, a clear conscience, and true happiness.—2 Corinthians 7:1.

HAPPINESS IN MARRIAGE

[11] Those living together as husband and wife should make sure that their marriage has been properly registered with the civil authorities. (Mark 12:17) They also need to view wedlock as a serious responsibility. True separation might become necessary in cases of willful nonsupport, extreme abuse, or the absolute endangerment of spirituality. (1 Timothy 5:8; Galatians 5:19-21) But the apostle Paul's words at 1 Corinthians 7:10-17 encourage marriage mates to stay together. For true happiness, of course, they must be faithful to each other. Paul wrote: "Let marriage be honorable among all, and the marriage bed be without defilement, for God will judge fornicators and adulterers." (Hebrews 13:4) The term "marriage bed" denotes sexual intercourse between a man and woman legally married to each other. No other sexual relationship, such as marriage to more than one wife, can be described as "honorable among all." Moreover, the Bible condemns premarital intercourse and homosexuality.—Romans 1:26, 27; 1 Corinthians 6:18.

[12] Fornication may bring a few moments of physical pleasure, but it does not result in true happiness. It dis-

---

11. What is required to have a legal and lasting honorable marriage?
12. What are some of the bad fruits of fornication?

leases God and can scar the person's conscience. (1 Thessalonians 4:3-5) The sad consequences of illegitimate sex may be AIDS and other sexually transmitted diseases. It has been estimated that more than 250 million people worldwide are infected annually with gonorrhoea, and about 50 million with syphilis," states one medical report. There is also the problem of unwanted pregnancies. The International Planned Parenthood Federation reports that, around the world, more than 15 million girls between the ages of 15 and 19 become pregnant each year, and a third of them have abortions. A study showed that in one African country, abortion complications result in 2 percent of all deaths among teenage girls. Some fornicators may escape disease and pregnancy but not emotional damage. Many lose their self-respect and even hate themselves.

[13] Although adultery may be forgiven, it is a valid Scriptural basis for divorce on the part of the innocent mate. Matthew 5:32; compare Hosea 3:1-5.) When such immorality results in the breakup of a marriage, this may leave deep emotional scars on the innocent mate and on the children. For the good of the human family, God's Word points out that his adverse judgment will come upon unrepentant fornicators and adulterers. Moreover, it clearly shows that those who practice sexual immorality "will not inherit God's kingdom."—Galatians 5:19, 21.

"NO PART OF THE WORLD"

[14] Those desiring to please Jehovah and enjoy Kingdom blessings avoid idolatry in any form. The Bible shows that it is wrong to make and worship images, including those of Christ, or of Jesus' mother, Mary. (Exodus 20:4, 5;

---

3. What additional problems are caused by adultery, and what lies ahead for those who continue to be fornicators and adulterers?
4. (a) What are some forms of idolatry that are avoided by a godly person? (b) What guidance is provided at John 17:14 and Isaiah 2:4?

1 John 5:21) So, true Christians do not venerate icons
crosses, and images. They also avoid more subtle form
of idolatry, such as acts of devotion to flags and the sing
ing of songs that glorify nations. When pressured to per
form such acts, they recall Jesus' words to Satan: "It is Je
hovah your God you must worship, and it is to him alon
you must render sacred service." (Matthew 4:8-10) Jesu
said that his followers are "no part of the world." (Joh
17:14) This means being neutral in political affairs and liv
ing peacefully in harmony with Isaiah 2:4, which says: "H
[Jehovah God] will certainly render judgment among the
nations and set matters straight respecting many peoples
And they will have to beat their swords into plowshare
and their spears into pruning shears. Nation will not lif
up sword against nation, neither will they learn war any
more."

¹⁵ Being "no part of the world" also means breaking off ll association with "Babylon the Great," the world em-ire of false religion. Unclean worship spread from an-ient Babylon until it held harmful spiritual dominion ver people earth wide. "Babylon the Great" embraces all eligions whose doctrines and practices are out of harmo-y with the knowledge of God. (Revelation 17:1, 5, 15) No aithful worshiper of Jehovah will engage in interfaith ac-ivities by sharing in worship with different religions or by aving spiritual fellowship with any part of Babylon the Great. (Numbers 25:1-9; 2 Corinthians 6:14) Consequent-y, many new Bible students send a letter of resignation to he religious organization to which they belong. This has rought them closer to the true God, as promised: "'Get

5. What is Babylon the Great, and what do many new Bible stu-ents do to get out of her?

Spiritual activities balanced with periods of relaxation contribute to the happiness of those living a godly life

out from among them, and separate yourselves,' says Je
hovah, 'and quit touching the unclean thing'; 'and I wi
take you in.'" (2 Corinthians 6:17; Revelation 18:4, 5)
not such acceptance by our heavenly Father what yo
keenly desire?

WEIGHING ANNUAL OBSERVANCES

¹⁶ A godly life frees us from the often burdensome cele
brating of worldly holidays. For instance, the Bible doe
not reveal the exact day of Jesus' birth. 'I thought Jesu
was born on December 25!' some may exclaim. This is no
possible because he died in the *spring* of 33 C.E. at 33 1/
years of age. Moreover, at the time of his birth, shepherd
were "living out of doors and keeping watches in the nigh
over their flocks." (Luke 2:8) In the land of Israel, late De
cember is a cold, rainy season during which sheep woul
be kept in shelters overnight to protect them from th
winter weather. Actually, December 25 was set aside b
the Romans as the birthday of their sun god. Centuries af
ter Jesus was on earth, apostate Christians adopted thi
date for the celebration of Christ's birth. Consequently
true Christians do not celebrate Christmas or any othe
holiday based on false religious beliefs. Because they giv
Jehovah exclusive devotion, they also do not observe hol
idays that idolize sinful humans or nations.

¹⁷ The Bible specifically mentions only two birthday ob
servances, both involving men who did not serve God
(Genesis 40:20-22; Matthew 14:6-11) Since the Scripture
do not reveal the birth date of the perfect man Jesu
Christ, why should we give special attention to the birth
days of imperfect humans? (Ecclesiastes 7:1) Of course
godly parents do not await a special day to show their chil
dren love. A 13-year-old Christian girl remarked: "My fam

16. Why do true Christians not celebrate Christmas?
17. Why do godly people not hold birthday parties, and why are
Christian children happy anyway?

ly and I have lots of fun. . . . I'm very close to my parents, and when other kids ask why I don't celebrate holidays, I tell them that I celebrate every day." Said a Christian youth aged 17: "In our house, gift-giving is all year long." Greater happiness results when gifts are given spontaneously.

¹⁸ For those pursuing a godly life, there is one day each year to be specially observed. It is the Lord's Evening Meal, often called the Memorial of Christ's death. Concerning it, Jesus commanded his followers: "Keep doing this in remembrance of me." (Luke 22:19, 20; 1 Corinthians 11:23-25) When Jesus instituted this meal on the night of Nisan 14, 33 C.E., he used unleavened bread and red wine, representing his sinless human body and his perfect blood. (Matthew 26:26-29) These emblems are partaken of by Christians anointed with God's holy spirit. They have been taken into the new covenant and the covenant for the Kingdom, and they have a heavenly hope. (Luke 12:32; 22:20, 28-30; Romans 8:16, 17; Revelation 14: 1-5) Nevertheless, benefits are experienced by all those present on the evening that corresponds with Nisan 14 on the ancient Jewish calendar. They are reminded of the love shown by Jehovah God and Jesus Christ in the sin-atoning ransom sacrifice that makes eternal life possible for those having divine favor.—Matthew 20:28; John 3:16.

EMPLOYMENT AND ENTERTAINMENT

¹⁹ True Christians are under obligation to work hard and provide for their needs. Accomplishing this brings family heads a feeling of satisfaction. (1 Thessalonians 4: 11, 12) Of course, if a Christian's employment conflicted with the Bible, this would rob him of happiness. Yet, it is sometimes difficult for a Christian to find employment that is in harmony with Bible standards. For instance,

18. What one annual observance did Jesus command his followers to keep, and of what does it remind us?
19. What challenge do Christians face in earning a living?

some employees are required to deceive customers. On the other hand, many employers will make concessions to accommodate the conscience of an honest worker, not wanting to lose a trustworthy employee. Whatever develops, however, you can be sure that God will bless your efforts to find employment that leaves you with a clean conscience.—2 Corinthians 4:2.

[20] Since God wants his servants to be happy, we need to balance hard work with refreshing periods of recreation and rest. (Mark 6:31; Ecclesiastes 3:12, 13) Satan's world promotes ungodly entertainment. But to please God, we must be selective about books we read, radio programs and music we listen to, and concerts, films, plays, television programs, and videos we watch. If the entertainment we chose in the past conflicts with the warnings in such scriptures as Deuteronomy 18:10-12, Psalm 11:5, and Ephesians 5:3-5, we will please Jehovah and will be happier if we make adjustments.

RESPECT FOR LIFE AND BLOOD

[21] For true happiness, we need to view human life as sacred, even as Jehovah does. His Word forbids us to commit murder. (Matthew 19:16-18) In fact, God's Law to Israel shows that he views the fetus as a precious life—not something to be destroyed. (Exodus 21:22, 23) For that matter, we must not treat life as something cheap by using tobacco, abusing our body with drugs or alcohol, or taking needless risks. Neither should we engage in any life-threatening pursuits nor should we ignore safety precautions, which might result in bloodguilt.—Deuteronomy 22:8.

[22] Jehovah told Noah and his family that blood represents the soul, or life. Therefore, God forbade them to eat

---

20. Why should we be selective in choosing entertainment?
21. How should respect for life affect our view of abortion, as well as our habits and conduct?
22. (a) What is the godly view of blood and its use? (b) Whose blood alone is truly lifesaving?

any blood. (Genesis 9:3, 4) Since we are their descendants, that law is binding upon all of us. Jehovah told the Israelites that blood was to be poured out on the ground and was not to be used for man's own purposes. (Deuteronomy 12:15, 16) And God's law on blood was reiterated when first-century Christians were instructed: "Keep abstaining . . . from blood." (Acts 15:28, 29) Out of respect for the sanctity of life, godly people do not accept blood transfusions, even if others insist that such a procedure would be lifesaving. Many medical alternatives acceptable to Jehovah's Witnesses have proved to be very effective and do not expose one to the hazards of blood transfusions. Christians know that only Jesus' shed blood is truly lifesaving. Faith in it brings forgiveness and the prospect of eternal life.—Ephesians 1:7.

23 Clearly, living a godly life requires effort. It may result in ridicule from family members or acquaintances. (Matthew 10:32-39; 1 Peter 4:4) But the rewards of living such a life far outweigh any trials. It results in a clean conscience and provides wholesome companionship with fellow worshipers of Jehovah. (Matthew 19:27, 29) Then, too, imagine living forever in God's righteous new world. (Isaiah 65:17, 18) And what joy there is in complying with Bible counsel and thus making Jehovah's heart rejoice! (Proverbs 27:11) No wonder that living a godly life brings happiness!—Psalm 128:1, 2.

23. What are some rewards of a godly way of life?

TEST YOUR KNOWLEDGE

What are some reasons why living a
godly life brings happiness?
•
Godly living may call for what changes?
•
Why do you want to live a godly life?

CHAPTER 14

WHOSE AUTHORITY SHOULD YOU RECOGNIZE?

"AUTHORITY" is a distasteful word to many people. This is understandable, for authority is often abused—on the job, in the family, and by governments. The Bible realistically says: "Man has dominated man to his injury." (Ecclesiastes 8:9) Yes, many have dominated others by acting in a tyrannical and self-serving manner.

² But not all authority is injurious. For example, it might be said that our body exercises authority over us. It "orders" us to breathe, eat, drink, and sleep. Is this oppressive? No. Compliance with these demands is for our good. While submission to our bodily needs may be involuntary, there are other forms of authority that require our *willing* subjection. Consider some examples.

THE SUPREME AUTHORITY

³ Over 300 times in the Bible, Jehovah is called "Sovereign Lord." A sovereign is one who possesses supreme authority. What gives Jehovah the right to this status? Revelation 4:11 answers: "You are worthy, Jehovah, even our God, to receive the glory and the honor and the power, because you created all things, and because of your will they existed and were created."

1, 2. Are all forms of authority injurious? Explain.
3. Why is Jehovah rightfully called "Sovereign Lord"?

⁴ As our Creator, Jehovah has the right to exercise his authority as he chooses. This might seem frightening, especially when we consider that God has an "abundance of dynamic energy." He is called "God Almighty"—a term that in Hebrew conveys the idea of overpowering strength. (Isaiah 40:26; Genesis 17:1) Yet, Jehovah shows his strength in a benevolent way, for his dominant quality is love.—1 John 4:16.

⁵ Although Jehovah warned that he would bring punishment upon unrepentant wrongdoers, Moses knew him principally as "the true God, the faithful God, keeping covenant and loving-kindness in the case of those who love him and those who keep his commandments." (Deuteronomy 7:9) Just imagine! The Supreme Authority of the universe does not force us to serve him. Rather, we are drawn to him because of his love. (Romans 2:4; 5:8) Submitting to Jehovah's authority is even a pleasure, for his laws always work to our ultimate benefit.—Psalm 19:7, 8.

⁶ Our first parents rejected God's sovereignty. They wanted to decide for themselves what was good and what was bad. (Genesis 3:4-6) As a result, they were ousted from their Paradise home. Jehovah thereafter allowed humans to create authority structures that would enable them to live in an orderly, though imperfect, society. What are some of these authorities, and to what degree does God expect us to submit to them?

"THE SUPERIOR AUTHORITIES"

⁷ The apostle Paul wrote: "Let every soul be in subjection to the superior authorities, for there is no authority

4. How does Jehovah choose to exercise his authority?
5. Why is it not difficult to submit to Jehovah's authority?
6. How did the issue of authority arise in the garden of Eden, and with what result?
7. Who are "the superior authorities," and how does their position relate to God's authority?

except by God." Who are the "superior authorities"? Paul's words in succeeding verses show that they are human governmental authorities. (Romans 13:1-7; Titus 3:1) Jehovah did not originate man's governmental authorities, but they exist by his permission. So Paul could write: "The existing authorities stand placed in their relative positions by God." What does this indicate about such earthly authority? That it is subordinate, or inferior, to God's authority. (John 19:10, 11) Therefore, when there is a conflict between man's law and God's law, Christians must be guided by their Bible-trained conscience. They "must obey God as ruler rather than men."—Acts 5:29.

⁸ Much of the time, however, the governmental superior authorities act as 'God's minister to us for our good.'

8. How do you benefit from the superior authorities, and how can you show your subjection to them?

(Romans 13:4) In what ways? Well, think of the numerous services the superior authorities provide, such as mail delivery, police and fire protection, sanitation, and education. "That is why you are also paying taxes," wrote Paul, "for they are God's public servants constantly serving this very purpose." (Romans 13:6) With regard to taxes or any other legal obligation, we should "conduct ourselves honestly."—Hebrews 13:18.

⁹ At times, the superior authorities misuse their power. Does this absolve us of our responsibility to remain in subjection to them? No, it does not. Jehovah sees the misdeeds of these authorities. (Proverbs 15:3) His toleration of man's rule does not mean that he winks at its corruption; nor does he expect us to do so. Indeed, God will soon "crush and put an end to all these kingdoms," replacing them with the rule of his own righteous government. (Daniel 2:44) But until this occurs, the superior authorities serve a useful purpose.

¹⁰ Paul explained: "He who opposes the authority has taken a stand against the arrangement of God." (Romans 13:2) The superior authorities are God's "arrangement" in that they preserve a measure of order, without which chaos and anarchy would reign. Opposing them would be unscriptural and senseless. To illustrate: Imagine that you had undergone surgery and stitches were securing the wound. Though the stitches are foreign to the body, they serve a purpose for a limited time. Removing them prematurely could be harmful. Similarly, human governmental authorities were not part of God's original purpose. Until his Kingdom is ruling the earth completely, however, human governments hold society together, performing a function that fits in with God's will for the present

9, 10. (a) How do the superior authorities fit into God's arrangement? (b) Why would it be wrong to oppose the superior authorities?

SUBMISSIVE, NOT SUBVERSIVE

Through their public preaching activity, Jehovah's Witnesses point to God's Kingdom as mankind's only hope for true peace and security. But these zealous proclaimers of God's Kingdom are by no means subversive to the governments under which they live. On the contrary, the Witnesses are among the most respectful and law-abiding of citizens. "If all the religious denominations were like Jehovah's witnesses," said an official in one African country, "we would have no murders, burglaries, delinquencies, prisoners and atomic bombs. Doors would not be locked day in and day out."

Recognizing this, officials in many lands have allowed the preaching work of the Witnesses to proceed unhindered. In other lands, bans or restrictions have been lifted when the authorities realized that Jehovah's Witnesses are an influence for the good. It is as the apostle Paul wrote about obeying the superior authorities: "Keep doing good, and you will have praise from it."—Romans 13:1, 3.

time. We should thus remain in subjection to the superior authorities, while we give priority to God's law and authority.

AUTHORITY IN THE FAMILY

¹¹ The family is the basic unit of human society. Within it a husband and a wife can find rewarding companionship, and children can be safeguarded and trained for adulthood. (Proverbs 5:15-21; Ephesians 6:1-4) Such a noble arrangement needs to be organized in a way that enables family members to live in peace and harmony. Jehovah's way of accomplishing this is through the principle of headship, summed up in these words, found at 1 Corinthians 11:3: "The head of every man is the Christ; in turn the head of a woman is the man; in turn the head of the Christ is God."

¹² The husband is the family head. However, there is a

---

11. How would you explain the principle of headship?
12, 13. Who is the family head, and what can be learned from Jesus' way of exercising headship?

head above him—Jesus Christ. Paul wrote: "Husbands, continue loving your wives, just as the Christ also loved the congregation and delivered up himself for it." (Ephesians 5:25) A husband reflects his subjection to Christ when he treats his wife in the way that Jesus has always treated the congregation. (1 John 2:6) Great authority has been conferred upon Jesus, but he exercises it with the utmost gentleness, love, and reasonableness. (Matthew 20:25-28) As a man, Jesus never abused his position of authority. He was "mild-tempered and lowly in heart," and he called his followers "friends" rather than "slaves." "I will refresh you," he promised them, and that is what he did.—Matthew 11:28, 29; John 15:15.

¹³ Jesus' example teaches husbands that Christian headship is not a position of harsh domination. Instead, it is one of respect and self-sacrificing love. This would clearly rule out mistreating a mate physically or verbally. (Ephesians 4:29, 31, 32; 5:28, 29; Colossians 3:19) If a Christian man were thus to mistreat his wife, his other good works would be valueless, and his prayers would be hindered. —1 Corinthians 13:1-3; 1 Peter 3:7.

¹⁴ When a husband imitates Christ's example, it is easier for his wife to comply with the words of Ephesians 5:22, 23: "Let wives be in subjection to their husbands as to the Lord, because a husband is head of his wife as the Christ also is head of the congregation." Just as a husband is to be submissive to Christ, a wife must be in subjection to her husband. The Bible also makes it clear that capable wives merit honor and praise for their godly wisdom and industriousness.—Proverbs 31:10-31.

¹⁵ A Christian wife's subjection to her husband is relative. This means that God rather than man must be obeyed if submitting in a certain matter would result in

14, 15. How does the knowledge of God help a wife to be submissive to her husband?

violating divine law. Even then, a wife's firm stand should be tempered with a "quiet and mild spirit." It should be evident that the knowledge of God has made her a better wife. (1 Peter 3:1-4) The same would be true of a Christian man whose wife is an unbeliever. His compliance with Bible principles should make him a better husband.

[16] Ephesians 6:1 outlines the role of children, stating: "Be obedient to your parents in union with the Lord, for this is righteous." Christian children follow the example of Jesus, who remained subject to his parents as he grew up. As an obedient boy, he "went on progressing in wisdom and in physical growth and in favor with God and men."—Luke 2:51, 52.

[17] The way parents handle their responsibilities may have a bearing on whether their children will respect authority or will rebel against it. (Proverbs 22:6) So parents might well ask themselves, 'Do I exercise my authority lovingly or harshly? Am I permissive?' A godly parent is expected to be loving and considerate, yet firm in adhering to godly principles. Appropriately, Paul wrote: "Fathers, do not be irritating your children [literally, 'provoking them to wrath'], but go on bringing them up in the discipline and mental-regulating of Jehovah."—Ephesians 6:4; Colossians 3:21.

[18] Parents should scrutinize their training methods, especially if they desire that their children be obedient and thus bring them joy. (Proverbs 23:24, 25) In the Bible, discipline is primarily a form of instruction. (Proverbs 4:1; 8:33) It is linked with love and mildness, not with anger and brutality. Hence, Christian parents need to act with

16. How can children imitate the example Jesus set when he was a youth?
17. The way parents exercise authority may have what effect on their children?
18. How should parental discipline be administered?

wisdom and keep themselves under restraint when disciplining their children.—Proverbs 1:7.

AUTHORITY IN THE CONGREGATION

¹⁹ Since Jehovah is an orderly God, it is reasonable that he would provide authoritative and well-organized leadership for his people. Accordingly, he has appointed Jesus as the Head of the Christian congregation. (1 Corinthians 14:33, 40; Ephesians 1:20-23) Under Christ's invisible leadership, God has authorized an arrangement by which appointed elders in each congregation shepherd the flock eagerly, willingly, and lovingly. (1 Peter 5:2, 3) Ministerial servants assist them in various ways and render valuable service within the congregation.—Philippians 1:1.

²⁰ Regarding Christian elders, Paul wrote: "Be obedient to those who are taking the lead among you and be submissive, for they are keeping watch over your souls as those who will render an account; that they may do this with joy and not with sighing, for this would be damaging to you." (Hebrews 13:17) Wisely, God has entrusted to Christian overseers the responsibility to care for the spiritual needs of those in the congregation. These elders do not constitute a clergy class. They are servants and slaves of God, ministering to the needs of their fellow worshipers, just as our Master, Jesus Christ, did. (John 10:14, 15) Knowing that Scripturally qualified men take an interest in our progress and spiritual growth encourages us to be cooperative and submissive.—1 Corinthians 16:16.

²¹ At times, sheep may stray or become endangered by harmful worldly elements. Under the leadership of

---

19. How has God provided for good order in the Christian congregation?
20. Why should we be submissive to appointed Christian elders, and why is this beneficial?
21. How do appointed elders seek to help fellow Christians spiritually?

the Chief Shepherd, elders as undershepherds are alert
to the needs of those in their charge and diligently give
them personal attention. (1 Peter 5:4) They visit members of the congregation and offer words of encouragement. Knowing that the Devil seeks to disrupt the peace
of God's people, elders exercise the wisdom from above
in dealing with any problems. (James 3:17, 18) They work
hard to maintain unity and oneness of faith, something
for which Jesus himself prayed.—John 17:20-22; 1 Corinthians 1:10.

²² What if a Christian suffers some evil or becomes dis-
couraged because of committing a sin? Soothing Bible
counsel and the elders' heartfelt prayers in his behalf can
help to restore him to spiritual health. (James 5:13-15)
These men, appointed by holy spirit, also have the authority to administer discipline and reprove any who pursue a
course of wrongdoing or who pose a danger to the spiritual and moral cleanness of the congregation. (Acts 20:28;
Titus 1:9; 2:15) In order to keep the congregation clean, it
may be necessary for individuals to report serious wrongdoing. (Leviticus 5:1) If a Christian who has committed
a grave sin accepts Scriptural discipline and reproof and
gives evidence of genuine repentance, he will be helped.
Of course, persistent and unrepentant violators of God's
law are disfellowshipped.—1 Corinthians 5:9-13.

²³ The Bible foretold that under Jesus Christ as King,
spiritually mature men would be appointed to provide
comfort, protection, and refreshment for God's people.
(Isaiah 32:1, 2) They would take the lead as evangeliz-
ers, shepherds, and teachers in order to promote spiritual
growth. (Ephesians 4:11, 12, 16) Although Christian overseers may at times reprove, reprimand, and exhort fel-

_____

22. What help do the elders provide in cases of wrongdoing?
23. What do Christian overseers provide for the good of the congregation?

low believers, application of the elders' healthful teaching
based on God's Word helps to keep all on the road to life.
—Proverbs 3:11, 12; 6:23; Titus 2:1.

ACCEPT JEHOVAH'S VIEW OF AUTHORITY

²⁴ The first man and woman were tested over the issue
of subjection to authority. Not surprisingly, a similar test
faces us daily. Satan the Devil has promoted a spirit of rebellion among mankind. (Ephesians 2:2) The course of independence is made to appear enticingly superior to that
of subjection.

²⁵ We must, however, reject the world's rebellious spirit.
In doing so, we will find that godly subjection brings rich
rewards. For instance, we will avoid the anxieties and frus-
trations common to those who court trouble with the secular authorities. We will reduce the friction that is prevalent in many families. And we will enjoy the benefits of
warm, loving association with our Christian fellow believers. Most of all, our godly subjection will result in a good
relationship with Jehovah, the Supreme Authority.

24. Over what issue are we tested daily?
25. What are the benefits of rejecting the world's rebellious spirit and of being submissive to authority that God exercises or permits?

TEST YOUR KNOWLEDGE

How does Jehovah exercise his authority?

•

Who are "the superior authorities," and how do
we remain in subjection to them?

•

What responsibility does the principle of headship
place on each family member?

•

How can we show submission in the
Christian congregation?

CHAPTER 15

BUILDING A FAMILY THAT HONORS GOD

SUPPOSE you plan to build your own home. You purchase the land. With keen anticipation, you see your new house in your mind's eye. But what if you have no tools and no building skills? How frustrating your efforts would be!

[2] Many couples enter marriage envisioning a happy family, yet possess neither the tools nor the skills needed to build one. Shortly after the wedding day, negative patterns develop. Fighting and bickering become a daily routine. When children are born, the new father and mother find themselves no more skilled at parenthood than they are at marriage.

[3] Happily, however, the Bible can help. Its principles are like tools that enable you to build a happy family. (Proverbs 24:3) Let us see how.

TOOLS FOR BUILDING A HAPPY MARRIAGE

[4] No matter how well-matched a married couple seem to be, they differ in emotional makeup, childhood experiences, and family background. Therefore, some problems are to be expected after marriage. How will they

---

1-3. Why are some unable to solve problems common to marriage and parenthood, but why can the Bible help?

4. Why are problems in marriage to be expected, and what standards are provided in the Bible?

be handled? Well, when builders construct a house, they consult the plans. These are guidelines to be followed. The Bible provides God's standards for building a happy family. Let us now examine a few of these.

⁵ *Loyalty.* Jesus said: "What God has yoked together let no man put apart."* (Matthew 19:6) The apostle Paul wrote: "Let marriage be honorable among all, and the marriage bed be without defilement, for God will judge fornicators and adulterers." (Hebrews 13:4) Married persons should therefore feel an obligation toward Jehovah to remain faithful to their mates.—Genesis 39:7-9.

⁶ Loyalty accords the marriage dignity and security. Loyal spouses know that, come what may, they will support each other. (Ecclesiastes 4:9-12) How different from those who abandon their marriage at the first hint of trouble! Such individuals quickly conclude that they 'chose the wrong person,' that they have 'fallen out of love,' that a new mate is the cure. But this gives neither spouse opportunity to grow. Instead, such disloyal ones may carry the same problems to new partners. When a person has a fine home but finds that the roof is leaking, surely he tries to repair it. He does not just move to another house. Similarly, changing a mate is not the way to solve the issues that lie beneath marital strife. When problems arise, do not try to get out of the marriage, but work very hard to preserve it. Such loyalty treats the union as something worth guarding, maintaining, and cherishing.

---

* The only Scriptural ground for divorce allowing for remarriage is "fornication"—sex relations outside the marriage.—Matthew 19:9.

---

5. How does the Bible stress the importance of loyalty in marriage?

6. How will loyalty help to preserve a marriage?

⁷ *Communication.* "There is a frustrating of plans where there is no confidential talk," says a Bible proverb. (Proverbs 15:22) Yet, communicating is difficult for some married couples. Why is that the case? Because people have different communication styles. This is a fact that often leads to considerable misunderstanding and frustration. Upbringing may play a role in this. For example, some may have been raised in an atmosphere of parental bickering. Now as married adults, they may not know how to speak to their mate in a kind and loving way. Nevertheless, your home need not deteriorate into 'a house full of quarreling.' (Proverbs 17:1) The Bible stresses putting on "the new personality," and it does not condone malicious bitterness, screaming, and abusive speech.—Ephesians 4:22-24, 31.

7. Why is communication often difficult for married people, but how can putting on "the new personality" help?

⁸ What can you do when there are disagreements? If tempers begin to flare, you may do well to follow the advice of Proverbs 17:14: "Before the quarrel has burst forth, take your leave." Yes, you might suspend the discussion until later, when both you and your mate have cooled off. (Ecclesiastes 3:1, 7) In any case, endeavor to be "swift about hearing, slow about speaking, slow about wrath." (James 1:19) Your goal should be to remedy the situation, not to win the argument. (Genesis 13:8, 9) Choose words and a manner of speaking that will calm you and your mate. (Proverbs 12:18; 15:1, 4; 29:11) Above all, do not remain in a provoked state, but seek help by communicating with God in humble prayer together.—Ephesians 4:26, 27; 6:18.

⁹ A Bible proverb says: "The heart of the wise one causes his mouth to show insight, and to his lips it adds persuasiveness." (Proverbs 16:23) Really, then, the key to successful communication is in the heart, not in the mouth. What is your attitude toward your mate? The Bible encourages Christians to show "fellow feeling." (1 Peter 3:8) Can you do this when your marriage partner experiences distressing anxiety? If so, it will help you to know how to answer.—Isaiah 50:4.

¹⁰ *Honor and Respect.* Christian husbands are told to dwell with their wives "according to knowledge, assigning them honor as to a weaker vessel, the feminine one." (1 Peter 3:7) Honoring one's wife involves recognizing her value. A husband who dwells with his wife "according to knowledge" has high regard for her feelings, strengths, intelligence, and dignity. He should also want

8. What may be helpful when you disagree with your mate?
9. Why can it be said that communication begins in the heart?
10, 11. How can a husband apply the counsel of 1 Peter 3:7?

to learn how Jehovah views women and wants them to
be treated.

¹¹ In your house, let us say that you have a very useful
container that is especially delicate. Would you not treat
it with great care? Well, Peter used the term "weaker vessel" in a similar vein, and this should move a Christian
husband to manifest tender regard for his beloved wife.

¹² But what counsel does the Bible give a wife? Paul
wrote: "The wife should have deep respect for her husband." (Ephesians 5:33) Just as a wife needs to sense
that she is honored and dearly loved by her mate, a husband needs to feel that he is respected by his wife. A respectful wife would not thoughtlessly broadcast her husband's faults, whether he is a Christian or not. She would
not strip him of his dignity by criticizing and belittling
him either privately or publicly.—1 Timothy 3:11; 5:13.

¹³ This does not mean that a wife cannot express her
opinions. If something disturbs her, she can respectfully
give voice to it. (Genesis 21:9-12) Conveying an idea to
her husband might be likened to throwing a ball to him.
She can toss it gently so that he can easily catch it, or
she can fling it with such force that it injures him. How
much better it is when both mates avoid hurling accu-
sations but, rather, speak in a kind and gentle manner!
—Matthew 7:12; Colossians 4:6; 1 Peter 3:3, 4.

¹⁴ As we have seen, Bible principles can help you to
build a happy marriage. But what if your mate shows little interest in what the Bible has to say? Much can still
be accomplished if you apply the knowledge of God in
your role. Peter wrote: "You wives, be in subjection to

12. How can a wife show that she deeply respects her husband?
13. How can viewpoints be expressed in a peaceable manner?
14. What should you do if your mate shows little interest in applying Bible principles in marriage?

your own husbands, in order that, if any are not obedient to the word, they may be won without a word through the conduct of their wives, because of having been eye-witnesses of your chaste conduct together with deep respect." (1 Peter 3:1, 2) Of course, the same would apply to a husband whose wife is indifferent toward the Bible. Regardless of what your mate chooses to do, let Bible principles make *you* a better spouse. The knowledge of God can also make you a better parent.

REARING CHILDREN ACCORDING TO THE KNOWLEDGE OF GOD

[15] Merely possessing a saw or a hammer does not make one a skilled carpenter. Likewise, simply having children does not make one a skilled parent. Knowingly or unknowingly, parents often bring up their children the way they themselves were brought up. Thus, faulty parenting techniques are sometimes passed on from one generation to the next. An ancient Hebrew proverb says: "Fathers are the ones that eat unripe grapes, but it is the teeth of the sons that get set on edge." Yet, the Scriptures show that a person does not have to follow the course set out by his parents. He can choose a different path, one influenced by Jehovah's statutes.—Ezekiel 18: 2, 14, 17.

[16] Jehovah expects Christian parents to give their children proper guidance and care. Paul wrote: "Certainly if anyone does not provide for those who are his own, and especially for those who are members of his household, he has disowned the faith and is worse than a person

15. How are faulty parenting techniques sometimes passed on, but how might this cycle be broken?
16. Why is it important to provide for your family, and what does this include?

without faith." (1 Timothy 5:8) What strong words! Fulfilling your role as a provider, which includes caring for your children's physical, spiritual, and emotional needs, is a godly person's privilege and responsibility. The Bible furnishes principles that can help parents build a happy environment for their children. Consider some of these.

[17] *Set a fine example.* Israelite parents were commanded: "You must inculcate [God's words] in your son and speak of them when you sit in your house and when you walk on the road and when you lie down and when you get up." Parents were to teach God's standards to their children. But this injunction was prefaced by the statement: "These words that I am commanding you today must prove to be on *your heart.*" (Deuteronomy 6:6, 7) Yes, parents cannot give what they do not have. God's laws must first be inscribed on your own hearts if you want to have them written on the hearts of your children.—Proverbs 20:7; compare Luke 6:40.

[18] *Provide assurance of your love.* At Jesus' baptism, Jehovah declared: "You are my Son, the beloved; I have approved you." (Luke 3:22) Jehovah thus acknowledged his Son, freely expressing approval of him and giving assurance of His love. Jesus later said to his Father: "You loved me before the founding of the world." (John 17:24) As godly parents, then, give your children verbal and physical expressions of your love for them—and do this often. Always remember that "love builds up."—1 Corinthians 8:1.

---

17. What is necessary if your children are to have God's law in their hearts?

18. In expressing love, how has Jehovah set a superb example for parents?

[19] *Discipline.* The Bible stresses the importance of loving discipline. (Proverbs 1:8) Parents who shirk their responsibility to guide their children today will almost certainly face heartbreaking consequences tomorrow. Yet, parents are also cautioned against going to the other extreme. "You fathers," wrote Paul, "do not be exasperating your children, so that they do not become downhearted." (Colossians 3:21) Parents must avoid overcorrecting their children or constantly harping on their shortcomings and criticizing their efforts.

[20] Jehovah God, our heavenly Father, sets the example in providing discipline. His correction is never extreme. "I shall have to chastise you to the proper degree," God told his people. (Jeremiah 46:28) Parents should imitate Jehovah in this regard. Discipline that exceeds reasonable limits or that goes beyond the intended purpose of correcting and teaching surely is exasperating.

[21] How can parents determine whether their discipline is effective? They might ask themselves, 'What does my discipline accomplish?' It should teach. Your child should understand why discipline is being administered. Parents should also be concerned about the aftereffects of their correction. True, almost all children will at first chafe at discipline. (Hebrews 12:11) But discipline should never make a child feel frightened or abandoned or leave him with the impression that he is inherently wicked. Before correcting his people, Jehovah said: "Do not be afraid, . . . for I am with you." (Jeremiah 46:28) Yes, correction should be administered in such a way that your child senses that you are with him or her as loving, supportive parents.

19, 20. What is involved in the proper disciplining of children, and how can parents benefit from Jehovah's example?
21. How can parents determine whether their discipline is effective?

ACQUIRING "SKILLFUL DIRECTION"

²² We can be grateful that Jehovah has provided the tools we need to build a happy family. But simply possessing the tools is not enough. We must practice using them properly. For example, a builder may develop poor habits in the way that he handles his tools. He may put some of them to a wrong use altogether. Under these circumstances, his methods are very likely to result in an inferior product. Similarly, you may now be aware of unhealthy habits that have crept into your family. Some may be strongly entrenched and hard to change. However, follow the Bible's advice: "A wise person will listen and take in more instruction, and a man of understanding is the one who acquires skillful direction."—Proverbs 1:5.

²³ You can acquire skillful direction by continuing to take in the knowledge of God. Be alert to Bible principles that apply to family life, and make adjustments where needed. Observe mature Christians who set a fine example as marriage mates and parents. Talk to them. Above all, take your concerns to Jehovah in prayer. (Psalm 55:22; Philippians 4:6, 7) He can help you to enjoy a happy family life that honors him.

22, 23. How can you acquire the direction needed to build a happy family?

TEST YOUR KNOWLEDGE

How do loyalty, communication, honor, and respect contribute to a happy marriage?

•

In what ways can parents assure their children of their love?

•

What factors are involved in proper discipline?

CHAPTER 16

HOW YOU CAN DRAW CLOSE TO GOD

A TOURIST visiting an Oriental country was amazed at the religious rituals she observed at a Buddhist temple. Although the images were not those of Mary or Christ, many of the rituals resembled those of her church back home. For instance, she noted the use of rosaries and the chanting of prayers. Others too have made such comparisons. East or West, the ways in which devotees try to draw close to God or to the objects of their worship are remarkably similar.

2 Many especially try to draw close to God by praying to him. Prayer has been described as "an act of communication by man with the sacred or holy—God, the gods, the transcendent realm, or supernatural powers." (*The New Encyclopædia Britannica*) When approaching God in prayer, however, some think only in terms of what they can get out of it. For example, a man once asked one of Jehovah's Witnesses: "If you pray for me, will the problems I have in my family, at work, and with my health be solved?" Apparently the man thought so, but many pray and find that their problems persist. So we might ask, 'Just why should we draw close to God?'

WHY DRAW CLOSE TO GOD

3 Prayer is not an empty ritual, nor is it merely a means

---

1. What similarities are evident in many religions?
2. How has prayer been described, and why do many people pray?
3. To whom should our prayers be directed, and why?

by which to gain something. A major reason for approaching God is to have a close relationship with him. Our prayers should therefore be directed to Jehovah God. "Jehovah is near to all those calling upon him," said the psalmist David. (Psalm 145:18) Jehovah invites us to come into a peaceful relationship with him. (Isaiah 1:18) Those responding to this invitation agree with the psalmist who said: "As for me, the drawing near to God is good for me." Why? Because those who draw near to Jehovah God will enjoy true happiness and peace of mind.—Psalm 73:28.

[4] Why pray to God for help if he 'knows what we need before we ask him'? (Matthew 6:8; Psalm 139:4) Prayer shows that we have faith in God and view him as the Source of "every good gift and every perfect present." (James 1:17; Hebrews 11:6) Jehovah takes pleasure in our prayers. (Proverbs 15:8) He is glad to hear our meaningful expressions of appreciation and praise, just as a father rejoices at hearing his young child speak sincere words of gratitude. (Psalm 119:108) Where there is a good father-child relationship, there is warm communication. A child who is loved wants to talk to his father. The same is true when it comes to our relationship with God. If we really appreciate what we are learning about Jehovah and the love he has shown for us, we will have a strong desire to express ourselves to him in prayer.—1 John 4:16-18.

[5] When approaching the Most High God, we should be respectful, though there is no need to worry excessively about the exact words that we use. (Hebrews 4:16) We always have access to Jehovah. And what a privilege it is that we can 'pour out our heart' to God in

---

4, 5. (a) Why is it important to pray to God? (b) What kind of relationship can we build with God through prayer?

prayer! (Psalm 62:8) Appreciation for Jehovah leads to a warm relationship with him, like the one that the faithful man Abraham enjoyed as God's friend. (James 2:23) But when praying to the Sovereign Lord of the universe, we must comply with his requirements for approaching him.

REQUIREMENTS FOR DRAWING CLOSE TO GOD

⁶ Is money needed in order to approach God? Many people pay the clergy to pray for them. Some even believe that their prayers will be heard in proportion to the size of the donation they make. However, God's Word does not say that a monetary offering is required for us to approach Jehovah in prayer. His spiritual provisions and the blessings of a relationship with him in prayer are available without price.—Isaiah 55:1, 2.

⁷ What, then, is required? A right heart attitude is one essential. (2 Chronicles 6:29, 30; Proverbs 15:11) In our heart we must exercise faith in Jehovah God as the "Hearer of prayer" and "the rewarder of those earnestly seeking him." (Psalm 65:2; Hebrews 11:6) We must also have a humble heart. (2 Kings 22:19; Psalm 51:17) In one of his illustrations, Jesus Christ showed that when approaching God a humble tax collector with a lowly heart attitude proved more righteous than an arrogant Pharisee. (Luke 18:10-14) As we approach God in prayer, let us remember that "everyone that is proud in heart is something detestable to Jehovah."—Proverbs 16:5.

⁸ If we desire to have God answer our prayers, we have to cleanse ourselves of sinful conduct. When the disciple

---

6, 7. Though God does not demand payment to hear our prayers, what does he require of us when we pray?

8. If we wish to have God answer our prayers, of what must we cleanse ourselves?

James encouraged others to draw close to God, he added: "Cleanse your hands, you sinners, and purify your hearts, you indecisive ones." (James 4:8) Even wrongdoers can come into a peaceful relationship with Jehovah if they repent and leave their former way of life. (Proverbs 28:13) We cannot have audience with Jehovah if we merely pretend that we have cleansed our way. "The eyes of Jehovah are upon the righteous ones, and his ears are toward their supplication; but the face of Jehovah is against those doing bad things," says God's Word.—1 Peter 3:12.

⁹ The Bible states: "There is no man righteous in the earth that keeps doing good and does not sin." (Ecclesiastes 7:20) You might therefore ask: 'How, then, can we approach Jehovah God?' The Bible answers: "If anyone does commit a sin, we have a helper with the Father, Jesus Christ, a righteous one." (1 John 2:1) Though we are sinners, we can approach God with freeness of speech through Jesus Christ, who died as a ransom for us. (Matthew 20:28) He is the only channel through whom we can approach Jehovah God. (John 14:6) We must not take the merit of Jesus' ransom sacrifice for granted and deliberately practice sin. (Hebrews 10:26) However, if we are doing our best to refrain from what is bad and yet err at times, we can repent and ask God for forgiveness. When we approach him with a humble heart, he will hear us.—Luke 11:4.

Opportunities to Talk to God

¹⁰ Jesus Christ valued his relationship with Jehovah

---

9. Through whom should we approach Jehovah, and why?
10. When it comes to prayer, how can we imitate Jesus, and what are some occasions for private prayer?

very highly. Therefore, Jesus made time to talk to God in private prayer. (Mark 1:35; Luke 22:40-46) We do well to imitate Jesus' example and pray to God on a regular basis. (Romans 12:12) It is fitting to start the day off with words of prayer, and before going to bed, we can rightly thank Jehovah for the day's activity. During the day, make it a point to approach God "on every occasion." (Ephesians 6:18) We can even pray silently in our heart, knowing that Jehovah can hear us. Privately talking to God helps us to cement our relationship with him, and praying to Jehovah daily helps us to draw ever closer to him.

¹¹ Jehovah also listens to prayers offered on behalf of groups of people. (1 Kings 8:22-53) We can draw close to God as a family, with the head of the household taking the lead. This strengthens the family bond, and Jehovah becomes real to young ones as they hear their parents humbly pray to God. What if someone is representing a group in prayer, perhaps at a meeting of Jehovah's Witnesses? If we are in the audience, let us listen attentively so that at the end of the prayer, we can wholeheartedly say "Amen," which means "So be it."—1 Corinthians 14:16.

PRAYERS THAT JEHOVAH HEARS

¹² Some may feel that God does not answer their prayers even though they pray to him through Christ. However, the apostle John said: "No matter what it is that we ask according to [God's] will, he hears us."

---

11. (a) Why should families pray together? (b) What does it mean when you say "Amen" at the end of a prayer?

12. (a) Why does God not answer some prayers? (b) Why should we not concentrate solely on personal needs when praying?

(1 John 5:14) So, then, we need to ask according to God's will. Since he is interested in our spiritual welfare, anything affecting our spirituality is an appropriate subject for prayer. We must resist the temptation to concentrate entirely on physical needs. For instance, while it is proper to pray for insight and fortitude to deal with illness, worries about health should not crowd out spiritual interests. (Psalm 41:1-3) Having become aware that she was overly concerned about her health, one Christian woman asked Jehovah for help to have the proper view of her illness. As a result, her health problems became a much smaller issue, and she felt that she was given "power beyond what is normal." (2 Corinthians 4:7) Her desire to be of spiritual help to others intensified, and she became a full-time Kingdom proclaimer.

¹³ What may we include in our prayers so that Jehovah will be pleased to hear them? Jesus Christ taught his disciples how to pray. In the model prayer recorded at Matthew 6:9-13, he set out a pattern of subjects about which we may rightly pray. What should be of chief concern in our prayers? Jehovah God's name and Kingdom must be the top priority. Asking for our material needs is appropriate. It is also important to ask for forgiveness of our sins and for deliverance from temptations and the wicked one, Satan the Devil. Jesus did not want us to chant this prayer or to repeat it over and over, reciting it without thinking about its meaning. (Matthew 6:7) What kind of relationship would it be if a child used the same words every time he spoke to his father?

¹⁴ Besides petitions and heartfelt supplications, we should offer prayers of praise and thanksgiving. (Psalm

13. As indicated at Matthew 6:9-13, what are some suitable subjects that we can include in our prayers?
14. Besides petitions, what prayers should we offer?

34:1; 92:1; 1 Thessalonians 5:18) We can also pray for
others. Prayers regarding our spiritual brothers and sis
ters who are afflicted or persecuted show our interest
in them, and Jehovah is pleased to hear us express such
concern. (Luke 22:32; John 17:20; 1 Thessalonians 5:25)
In fact, the apostle Paul wrote: "Do not be anxious
over anything, but in everything by prayer and supplica
tion along with thanksgiving let your petitions be made
known to God; and the peace of God that excels all
thought will guard your hearts and your mental powers
by means of Christ Jesus."—Philippians 4:6, 7.

PERSEVERE IN PRAYER

¹⁵ Though you are gaining knowledge about God, you
may feel that your prayers sometimes go unanswered.
This could be the case because it may not be God's time
to answer a specific prayer. (Ecclesiastes 3:1-9) Jehovah
may allow a situation to continue for a while, but he
does answer prayers and knows the best time to do so.
—2 Corinthians 12:7-9.

¹⁶ Our persistence in prayer reveals our heartfelt inter
est in what we are saying to God. (Luke 18:1-8) For ex
ample, we may ask Jehovah to help us overcome a cer
tain weakness. By persevering in prayer and acting in
harmony with our petitions, we show our sincerity. We
should be specific and honest in our petitions. It is es
pecially important to pray intensely when we are experi
encing a temptation. (Matthew 6:13) As we continue to
pray while trying to control our sinful urges, we will
see how Jehovah helps us. This will build up our faith

---

15. What should we remember if our prayers seem to go unanswered?

16. Why should we persist in prayer, and how can doing this affect
our relationship with God?

and strengthen our relationship with him.—1 Corinthi
ans 10:13; Philippians 4:13.

¹⁷ By cultivating a prayerful attitude in rendering sa
cred service to Jehovah God, we will come to realize
that we do not serve him in our own strength. It is Jeho
vah who gets things done. (1 Corinthians 4:7) Acknowl
edging this will help us to be humble and will enrich our
relationship with him. (1 Peter 5:5, 6) Yes, we have sound
reasons to persevere in prayer. Our earnest prayers and
precious knowledge of how to draw close to our loving
heavenly Father will make our life truly happy.

COMMUNICATION
WITH JEHOVAH NOT ONE-SIDED

¹⁸ If we want God to hear our prayers, we must listen
to what he says. (Zechariah 7:13) He no longer sends his
messages through divinely inspired prophets and surely
does not use spiritistic means. (Deuteronomy 18:10-12)
But we can listen to God by studying his Word, the Bi
ble. (Romans 15:4; 2 Timothy 3:16, 17) Just as we may
need to acquire a taste for physical food that is good for
us, we are urged to "form a longing for the unadulterat
ed milk belonging to the word." Cultivate a taste for spir
itual food by reading God's Word daily.—1 Peter 2:2, 3;
Acts 17:11.

¹⁹ Meditate on what you read in the Bible. (Psalm 1:
1-3; 77:11, 12) That means to ponder over the material.
You might liken this to digesting food. You can digest
spiritual food by relating what you are reading to things
you already know. Consider how the material affects
your life, or reflect on what it reveals about Jehovah's
qualities and dealings. Thus through personal study, you

17. How will we benefit from a prayerful attitude in serving God?
18. How can we listen to God?
19. Of what benefit is it to meditate on what you read in the Bible?

can take in the spiritual food that Jehovah provides. This will draw you closer to God and will help you to deal with day-to-day problems.

20 You can also draw close to God by listening to his Word discussed at Christian meetings, just as the Israelites listened attentively when they gathered to hear the public reading of God's Law. The instructors of that time put meaning into their reading of the Law, thus helping their listeners to understand and be moved to apply what they heard. This led to great joy. (Nehemiah 8:8, 12) So make it your custom to attend the meetings of Jehovah's Witnesses. (Hebrews 10:24, 25) This will help you to understand and then apply the knowledge of God in your life and will bring you happiness. Being a part of the worldwide Christian brotherhood will help you to stay close to Jehovah. And as we shall see, you can find true security among God's people.

20. How does attending Christian meetings help us to draw close to God?

TEST YOUR KNOWLEDGE

Why should you draw
close to Jehovah?
•
What are some requirements for
drawing close to God?
•
What can you include
in your prayers?
•
Why should you persevere
in prayer?
•
How can you listen
to Jehovah today?

CHAPTER 17

FIND SECURITY AMONG GOD'S PEOPLE

IMAGINE that a violent storm has ravaged the area where you live. Your home is destroyed, and all your possessions are lost. Food is scarce. The situation seems hopeless. Then, unexpected relief supplies arrive. Food and clothing are provided in abundance. A new house is built for you. Surely you would be grateful to the person who made these provisions available.

² Something comparable is occurring today. Like that storm, the rebellion of Adam and Eve caused great damage to the human race. Mankind's Paradise home was lost. Since then, human governments have failed to shelter people from war, crime, and injustice. Religion has left multitudes starving for wholesome spiritual food. Spiritually speaking, however, Jehovah God is now furnishing food, clothing, and shelter. How is he doing that?

"THE FAITHFUL AND DISCREET SLAVE"

³ Relief supplies are generally dispensed through an organized channel, and Jehovah has similarly made spiritual provision for his people. For example, the Israelites were "Jehovah's congregation" for some 1,500 years. Among them were those who served as God's channel to

---

1, 2. How is mankind's situation like that of people in a storm-ravaged area?

3. How does Jehovah supply provisions for mankind, as shown by what examples?

teach his Law. (1 Chronicles 28:8; 2 Chronicles 17:7-9) In the first century C.E., Jehovah brought forth the Christian organization. Congregations were formed, and they functioned under the direction of a governing body made up of apostles and older men. (Acts 15:22-31) Likewise today, Jehovah deals with his people through an organized body. How do we know this?

⁴ Jesus said that at the time of his presence in Kingdom power, "the faithful and discreet slave" would be found providing "food at the proper time" for His followers. (Matthew 24:45-47) When Jesus was installed as heavenly King in 1914, who did this "slave" prove to be? Certainly not the clergy of Christendom. For the most part, they were feeding their flocks propaganda that backed up their own national governments in World War I. But proper and timely spiritual food was being dispensed by the group of true Christians who were anointed by God's holy spirit and were a part of what Jesus called the "little flock." (Luke 12:32) These anointed Christians preached God's Kingdom rather than man's governments. As a result, over the years millions of righteously disposed "other sheep" have joined the anointed "slave" in practicing true religion. (John 10:16) Using the 'faithful slave' and its present-day Governing Body, God directs his organized people to make spiritual food, clothing, and shelter available to all who wish to have these provisions.

"FOOD AT THE PROPER TIME"

⁵ Jesus said: "Man must live, not on bread alone, but on every utterance coming forth through Jehovah's

---

4. Who has "the faithful and discreet slave" proved to be in modern times, and how are God's spiritual provisions made available?
5. What spiritual condition exists in the world today, but what is Jehovah doing about this?

mouth." (Matthew 4:4) Sadly, though, the vast majority
of people are not paying attention to God's utterances
As foretold by Jehovah's prophet Amos, there is "a fam
ine, not for bread, and a thirst, not for water, but fo
hearing the words of Jehovah." (Amos 8:11) Even very
religious people are spiritually famished. Nevertheless
Jehovah's will is that "all sorts of men should be saved
and come to an accurate knowledge of truth." (1 Timothy 2:3, 4) Accordingly, he is providing spiritual food in
abundance. But where can it be obtained?

⁶ Throughout history, Jehovah has dispensed spiritual food to his people as a group. (Isaiah 65:13) For instance, the Israelite priests gathered men, women, and
children for group instruction in God's Law. (Deuteronomy 31:9, 12) Under the direction of the governing body,
first-century Christians organized congregations and
held meetings for the instruction and encouragement of
all. (Romans 16:5; Philemon 1, 2) Jehovah's Witnesses
follow this pattern. You are cordially invited to attend all
their meetings.

⁷ Of course, you may already have learned much in
your personal study of the Bible. Perhaps someone has
assisted you. (Acts 8:30-35) But your faith might be likened to a plant that will wither and die if it is not given
suitable care. Hence, you must receive proper spiritual
nourishment. (1 Timothy 4:6) Christian meetings provide a continuous program of instruction designed to
nourish you spiritually and help you to keep on growing
in faith as you increase in the knowledge of God.—Colossians 1:9, 10.

---

6. How has Jehovah fed his people spiritually in times past?
7. How is regular attendance at Christian meetings related to
knowledge and faith?

⁸ Meetings serve another vital purpose. Paul wrote: "Let us consider one another to incite to love and fine works, not forsaking the gathering of ourselves together." (Hebrews 10:24, 25) The Greek word translated "to incite" can also mean "to sharpen." A Bible proverb states: "By iron, iron itself is sharpened. So one man sharpens the face of another." (Proverbs 27:17) All of us need continual 'sharpening.' Daily pressures from the world can dull our faith. When we attend Christian meetings, there is an interchange of encouragement. (Romans 1:11, 12) Members of the congregation follow the apostle Paul's admonition to "keep comforting one another and building one another up," and such things sharpen our faith. (1 Thessalonians 5:11) Regular presence at Christian meetings also indicates that we love God and affords us opportunities to praise him. —Psalm 35:18.

"CLOTHE YOURSELVES WITH LOVE"

⁹ Paul wrote: "Clothe yourselves with love, for it is a perfect bond of union." (Colossians 3:14) Jehovah has graciously provided this clothing for us. In what way? Christians can display love because it is one of the God-given fruits of Jehovah's holy spirit. (Galatians 5:22, 23) Jehovah himself has displayed the greatest love by sending his only-begotten Son so that we might have everlasting life. (John 3:16) This supreme demonstration of love provided a model for us in expressing this quality. "If this is how God loved us," wrote the apostle John, "then we are ourselves under obligation to love one another." —1 John 4:11.

---

8. Why are we encouraged to attend the meetings of Jehovah's Witnesses?
9. How has Jehovah set the example in displaying love?

¹⁰ Your attending the meetings at the Kingdom Hall will afford you an excellent opportunity to show love. There you will meet a wide variety of people. No doubt you will feel drawn to many of them right away. Of course, personalities differ even among those serving Jehovah. Perhaps in the past you simply avoided people who did not share your interests or traits. Christians, though, are to "have love for the *whole* association of brothers." (1 Peter 2:17) Therefore, make it your aim to become acquainted with those at the Kingdom Hall —even individuals whose age, personality, race, or level of education may differ from yours. Likely you will find that each one excels in some endearing quality.

¹¹ The diversity of personalities in the congregation need not disturb you. To illustrate, imagine that numerous vehicles are traveling alongside you on a road. Not all are moving at the same speed, nor are all in the same condition. Some have traveled many miles, but like you, others have just started out. Regardless of these differences, however, all are traveling down the road. It is similar with the individuals making up a congregation. Not all develop Christian qualities at the same speed. Furthermore, not all are in the same physical or emotional condition. Some have been worshiping Jehovah for many years; others have just begun. Yet, all are traveling along the road to everlasting life, "fitly united in the same mind and in the same line of thought." (1 Corinthians 1:10) Therefore, look for the strengths rather than the weaknesses of those in the congregation. Doing that will warm your heart, for you will realize that God is really among these people. And surely this is where you want to be.—1 Corinthians 14:25.

10. How can we benefit from "the *whole* association of brothers"?
11. Why should you not be disturbed by the variety of personalities among Jehovah's people?

¹² Since all humans are imperfect, at times someone in the congregation may say or do something that upsets you. (Romans 3:23) The disciple James realistically wrote: "We all stumble many times. If anyone does not stumble in word, this one is a perfect man." (James 3:2) How will you react if someone offends you? A Bible proverb says: "The insight of a man certainly slows down his anger, and it is beauty on his part to pass over transgression." (Proverbs 19:11) To have insight means to see beneath the surface of a situation, to grasp underlying factors that cause a person to talk or act in a certain way. Most of us use much insight in excusing our own mistakes. Why not also use it to understand and cover the imperfections of others?—Matthew 7:1-5; Colossians 3:13.

¹³ Never forget that we must forgive others if we ourselves are to receive Jehovah's forgiveness. (Matthew 6: 9, 12, 14, 15) If we are practicing the truth, we will treat others in a loving way. (1 John 1:6, 7; 3:14-16; 4:20, 21) Therefore, if you encounter a problem with an individual in the congregation, fight against harboring resentment. If you are clothed with love, you will strive to resolve the problem, and you will not hesitate to apologize if you have caused offense.—Matthew 5:23, 24; 18:15-17.

¹⁴ Our spiritual clothing should include other qualities closely related to love. Paul wrote: "Clothe yourselves with the tender affections of compassion, kindness, lowliness of mind, mildness, and long-suffering." These traits, encompassed by love, are part of the godly "new personality." (Colossians 3:10, 12) Will you make

---

12, 13. (a) If someone in the congregation offends you, what can you do? (b) Why is it important not to harbor resentment?
14. With what qualities should we be clothed?

the effort to clothe yourself in this way? Especially if you clothe yourself with brotherly love will you bear an identifying mark of Jesus' disciples, for he said: "By this all will know that you are my disciples, if you have love among yourselves."—John 13:35.

A PLACE OF SECURITY

15 The congregation also serves as a shelter, a protective refuge where you can feel secure. In it you will find honesthearted people who are striving to do what is right in God's eyes. Many of them have done away with the same bad practices and attitudes that you may be struggling to overcome. (Titus 3:3) They can help you, for we are told to "go on carrying the burdens of one another." (Galatians 6:2) Naturally, pursuing a course that leads to everlasting life is ultimately your own responsibility. (Galatians 6:5; Philippians 2:12) Yet, Jehovah has provided the Christian congregation as a wonderful means of help and support. No matter how distressing your problems may be, you have a valuable resource available to you—a loving congregation that will stand by you in times of affliction or deprivation.—Compare Luke 10:29-37; Acts 20:35.

16 Among those who would rally to your support are "gifts in men"—appointed congregation elders, or overseers, who shepherd the flock willingly and eagerly. (Ephesians 4:8, 11, 12; Acts 20:28; 1 Peter 5:2, 3) Regarding them, Isaiah prophesied: "Each one must prove to be like a hiding place from the wind and a place of concealment from the rainstorm, like streams of water in a waterless country, like the shadow of a heavy crag in an exhausted land."—Isaiah 32:2.

---

15. How is the congregation like a shelter?
16. What assistance do congregation elders provide?

[17] When Jesus was on earth, loving oversight by the religious leaders was sadly lacking. The condition of the people moved him deeply, and he especially wanted to help them spiritually. Jesus pitied them because "they were skinned and thrown about like sheep without a shepherd." (Matthew 9:36) How well this describes the present-day plight of many who endure heart-wrenching problems with no one to turn to for spiritual help and comfort! But Jehovah's people do have spiritual assistance, for he promised: "I will raise up over them shepherds who will actually shepherd them; and they will be afraid no more, neither will they be struck with any terror, and none will be missing."—Jeremiah 23:4.

[18] Get to know the appointed elders in the congregation. They have much experience in applying the knowledge of God, for they have met the qualifications for overseers set forth in the Bible. (1 Timothy 3:1-7; Titus 1: 5-9) Do not hesitate to approach one of them if you need spiritual help to overcome a habit or a trait that conflicts with God's requirements. You will find that the elders follow Paul's admonition: "Speak consolingly to the depressed souls, support the weak, be long-suffering toward all."—1 Thessalonians 2:7, 8; 5:14.

ENJOY SECURITY WITH JEHOVAH'S PEOPLE

[19] Though we now live amid imperfect conditions, Jehovah provides us with spiritual food, clothing, and shelter. Of course, we must wait for God's promised new world in order to experience the benefits of a physical paradise. But those who are part of Jehovah's organi-

---

17. (a) What sort of help did Jesus especially want to give?
(b) What provision did God promise to make for his people?
18. Why should we approach an elder if we need spiritual help?
19. What blessings has Jehovah bestowed upon those who seek security inside his organization?

zation are presently enjoying the security of a spiritual paradise. Concerning them, Ezekiel prophesied: "They will actually dwell in security, with no one to make them tremble."—Ezekiel 34:28; Psalm 4:8.

[20] How grateful we can be that Jehovah makes loving spiritual provisions through his Word and organization! Draw close to God's people. Do not hold back in fear of what friends or relatives may think of you for taking in the knowledge of God. Some may disapprove because you are associating with Jehovah's Witnesses and attending meetings at the Kingdom Hall. But God will more than compensate for anything you sacrifice for the sake of his worship. (Malachi 3:10) Moreover, Jesus said: "No one has left house or brothers or sisters or mother or father or children or fields for my sake and for the sake of the good news who will not get a hundredfold now in this period of time, houses and brothers and sisters and mothers and children and fields, with persecutions, and in the coming system of things everlasting life." (Mark 10:29, 30) Yes, no matter what you have left behind or must endure, you can find delightful companionship and spiritual security among God's people.

---

20. How will Jehovah compensate for anything we may sacrifice for the sake of his worship?

TEST YOUR KNOWLEDGE

Who is "the faithful and discreet slave"?

•

What provision has Jehovah made to feed us spiritually?

•

How can those in the Christian congregation help us?

CHAPTER 18

MAKE IT YOUR AIM TO SERVE GOD FOREVER

IMAGINE that you are standing before a locked door leading to a room containing great treasures. Let us say that an authorized person has given you the key and has told you to help yourself to these valuable things. That key will do you no good unless you use it. Similarly, you must use knowledge if it is to benefit you.

² This is particularly true of the knowledge of God. Indeed, accurate knowledge of Jehovah God and Jesus Christ means everlasting life. (John 17:3) Yet, that prospect cannot be realized through the mere possession of knowledge. As you would use a valued key, you need to apply the knowledge of God in your life. Jesus said that those *doing* God's will would "enter into the kingdom." Such individuals would be privileged to serve God forever!—Matthew 7:21; 1 John 2:17.

³ After learning what God's will is, it is vital to do it. What do you think that God's will is for you? It could well be summed up in these words: Imitate Jesus. First Peter 2:21 tells us: "To this course you were called, because even Christ suffered for you, leaving you a mod-

1, 2. What is required besides possession of the knowledge of God?
3. What is God's will for us?

el for you to follow his steps closely." To do God's will, then, you need to follow Jesus' example as closely as possible. That is how you put to use the knowledge of God.

HOW JESUS USED THE KNOWLEDGE OF GOD

⁴ Jesus Christ has a more intimate knowledge of God than others do. He lived and worked with Jehovah God in heaven for ages before coming to the earth. (Colossians 1:15, 16) And what did Jesus do with all that knowledge? He was not satisfied with merely possessing it. Jesus lived by it. That is why he was so kind, patient, and loving in his dealings with fellow humans. Jesus was thus imitating his heavenly Father and acting in harmony with his knowledge of Jehovah's ways and personality.—John 8: 23, 28, 29, 38; 1 John 4:8.

⁵ The knowledge Jesus had also moved him to take a crucial step. He came from Galilee to the Jordan River, where John baptized him. (Matthew 3:13-15) What did Jesus' baptism symbolize? As a Jew, he was born into a nation dedicated to God. Hence, Jesus had been dedicated from birth. (Exodus 19:5, 6) By submitting to baptism, he was *presenting* himself to Jehovah to do the divine will for him at that time. (Hebrews 10:5, 7) And Jesus lived up to the meaning of his baptism. He spent himself in Jehovah's service, sharing the knowledge of God with people at every opportunity. Jesus found delight in doing God's will, even saying that this was like food for him.—John 4:34.

⁶ Jesus fully realized that doing Jehovah's will would

---

4. Why does Jesus know so much about Jehovah, and how has he used this knowledge?

5. Why did Jesus get baptized, and how did he live up to the meaning of his baptism?

6. In what way did Jesus disown himself?

Have you made a dedication to God in prayer?

be very costly—that it would even cost him his life. Nevertheless, Jesus disowned himself, putting his personal needs in second place. Doing God's will always came first. In this respect, how can we follow Jesus' perfect example?

STEPS THAT LEAD TO LIFE ETERNAL

[7] Unlike Jesus, we are imperfect and can reach the milestone of baptism only after taking other vital steps. This begins by taking accurate knowledge of Jehovah God and Jesus Christ into our heart. Doing this causes us to exercise faith and to have profound love for God. (Matthew 22:37-40; Romans 10:17; Hebrews 11:6) Compliance with God's laws, principles, and standards should move us to repent, expressing godly sorrow over our past sins. This leads to conversion, that is, to a turning around and abandoning any wrong course we followed when we did not have the knowledge of God. (Acts 3:19) Naturally, if we are still secretly practicing some sin instead of doing what is righteous, we have not really turned around, nor have we fooled God. Jehovah detects all hypocrisy.—Luke 12:2, 3.

[8] Now that you have been taking in the knowledge of God, is it not fitting to consider spiritual matters in a very personal way? Probably you are eager to tell your relatives, friends, and others what you are learning. In fact, you may already have been doing this, even as Jesus shared the good news with others in informal settings. (Luke 10:38, 39; John 4:6-15) Now you may want to do more. Christian elders will be glad to talk with you in order to determine whether you are qualified and able to have some share in the regular Kingdom-preaching

7. What are some steps one must take to qualify for baptism?
8. What action should you take when you desire to share in the Kingdom-preaching activity?

*What prevents
you from getting
baptized?*

activity of Jehovah's Witnesses. If you are, the elders
will make arrangements for you to accompany a Witness in the ministry. Jesus' disciples followed his instructions in order to carry out their ministry in an orderly
way. (Mark 6:7, 30; Luke 10:1) You will benefit from similar help as you share in spreading the Kingdom message
from house to house and in other ways.—Acts 20:20, 21.

⁹ Preaching the good news to all kinds of people in
the congregation's territory is a way to find those who
are righteously disposed and is among the fine works
proving that you have faith. (Acts 10:34, 35; James 2:17,
18, 26) Regular attendance at Christian meetings and
having a meaningful share in the preaching work are
also ways to demonstrate that you have repented and
turned around and are now determined to live in accord
with the knowledge of God. What is the next logical
step? It is to make a dedication to Jehovah God. This
means that in heartfelt prayer, you tell God that you are
willingly and wholeheartedly giving your life to him to
do his will. This is the way to dedicate yourself to Jehovah and accept the kindly yoke of Jesus Christ.—Matthew 11:29, 30.

BAPTISM—WHAT IT MEANS FOR YOU

¹⁰ According to Jesus, all those who become his disciples must be baptized. (Matthew 28:19, 20) Why is
this necessary after you have made a dedication to God?
Since you have dedicated yourself to Jehovah, he knows
that you love him. But no doubt you will want to take
further action in order to let others know about your
love for God. Well, baptism affords you an opportunity

---

9. How does a person make a dedication to God, and how does
dedication affect the person's life?
10. Why should you get baptized after you dedicate yourself to Jehovah?

to make your dedication to Jehovah God known publicly.—Romans 10:9, 10.

[11] Baptism is rich in symbolic meaning. As you are sub-
merged, or "buried," beneath the water, it is as though
you have died to your former course of life. When you
come up out of the water, it is as if you are emerging to a
new life, one that is governed by God's will and not your
own. Of course, that does not mean that you will make no
more mistakes, for all of us are imperfect and therefore
sin daily. However, as a dedicated, baptized servant of Jehovah, you will have entered into a special relationship
with him. Because of your repentance and your humble
submission to baptism, Jehovah is willing to forgive your
sins on the basis of Jesus' ransom sacrifice. Baptism thus
leads to a clean conscience before God.—1 Peter 3:21.

[12] Jesus commanded his followers to baptize new disciples "in the name of the Father and of the Son and of the
holy spirit." (Matthew 28:19) What did Jesus mean? Baptism "in the name of the Father" indicates that the person being baptized wholeheartedly accepts Jehovah God
as the Creator and the rightful Sovereign of the universe.
(Psalm 36:9; 83:18; Ecclesiastes 12:1) Being baptized 'in
the name of the Son' means that the individual acknowl-
edges Jesus Christ—and particularly His ransom sacrifice—as the only means of salvation provided by God.
(Acts 4:12) Baptism 'in the name of the holy spirit' signifies that the baptismal candidate recognizes Jehovah's
holy spirit, or active force, as God's instrument for carrying out His purposes and for empowering His servants
to do His righteous will in association with His spirit-
directed organization.—Genesis 1:2; Psalm 104:30; John
14:26; 2 Peter 1:21.

---

11. What is the meaning of baptism?
12. What does it mean to be baptized (a) "in the name of the Father"? (b) 'in the name of the Son'? (c) 'in the name of the holy
spirit'?

ARE YOU READY FOR BAPTISM?

¹³ Since baptism means so much and is the most important milestone in a person's life, is it a step that you should fear? Not at all! While the decision to be baptized is not to be taken lightly, it is unquestionably the wisest one you could possibly make.

¹⁴ Baptism gives evidence of your choice to serve Jehovah God. Think about people with whom you come in contact. In one way or another, is not each one of them serving a master? Some slave for riches. (Matthew 6:24) Others diligently pursue their careers or serve themselves by making the fulfillment of their own desires paramount in life. Still others serve false gods. But you have chosen to serve the true God, Jehovah. No one else shows as much kindness, compassion, and love. God dignifies humans with purposeful work that points them to salvation. He rewards his servants with everlasting life. Surely, following Jesus' example and giving your life to Jehovah is not a course to fear. Actually, it is the only one that pleases God and makes perfect sense.—1 Kings 18:21.

¹⁵ Yet, baptism is not a step to be taken because of pressure. It is a personal matter between you and Jehovah. (Galatians 6:4) As you have made spiritual progress, you may have wondered: "What prevents me from getting baptized?" (Acts 8:35, 36) You might ask yourself, 'Is family opposition holding me back? Am I still involved in some unscriptural situation or sinful practice? Could it be that I am afraid of losing favor in the community?' These are some of the factors to consider, but weigh them realistically.

¹⁶ It is not realistic to weigh the costs without considering the benefits of serving Jehovah. For instance, consider

---

13, 14. Why should we not be afraid to choose to serve Jehovah God?

15. What are some common obstacles to baptism?

16. How will you benefit from serving Jehovah?

the matter of family opposition. Jesus promised that even if his disciples lost their relatives because of following him, they would gain a larger spiritual family. (Mark 10: 29, 30) These fellow believers will show you brotherly love, help you to endure persecution, and support you on the road to life. (1 Peter 5:9) Especially can the congregation elders help you to cope with problems and to meet other challenges successfully. (James 5:14-16) As to losing favor in this world, you may well ask yourself, 'What can possibly compare to having the approval of the Creator of the universe, causing him to rejoice over my chosen life course?'—Proverbs 27:11.

LIVING UP TO YOUR DEDICATION AND BAPTISM

¹⁷ It is important to remember that baptism is not the end of your spiritual progress. It marks the beginning of lifelong service to God as an ordained minister and one of Jehovah's Witnesses. Although baptism is vitally important, it is not a guarantee of salvation. Jesus did not say: 'Everyone baptized will be saved.' Instead, he said: "He that has endured to the end is the one that will be saved." (Matthew 24:13) Therefore, it is vital that you seek God's Kingdom first by making it the paramount concern in your life.—Matthew 6:25-34.

¹⁸ To endure in your service to Jehovah, you will want to set spiritual goals for yourself. One worthy goal is to further your knowledge of God through regular personal study of his Word. Plan for daily reading of the Bible. (Psalm 1:1, 2) Attend Christian meetings regularly, for the association you find there will help to give you spiritual strength. For your part, why not make it your goal to comment at congregation meetings and thus

17. Why should you view baptism as a beginning rather than an end?
18. After baptism, what are some goals to pursue?

praise Jehovah and seek to upbuild others? (Romans 1:
11, 12) Another goal might be to improve the quality of
your prayers.—Luke 11:2-4.

[19] If you are to live up to the meaning of your baptism, you need to pay constant attention to what you
do, letting God's holy spirit produce in you such qualities as love, joy, peace, long-suffering, kindness, goodness, faith, mildness, and self-control. (Galatians 5:22, 23;
2 Peter 3:11) Remember, Jehovah gives his holy spirit to
all who pray for it and obey him as his faithful servants.
(Luke 11:13; Acts 5:32) So pray to God for his spirit and
ask him for help in displaying qualities that please him.
Such qualities will become more evident in your speech
and conduct as you respond to the influence of God's
spirit. Of course, every individual in the Christian congregation is striving to develop "the new personality" so
as to become more like Christ. (Colossians 3:9-14) Each
one of us faces different challenges in doing this because
we are at varying stages of spiritual progress. Since you
are imperfect, you must work hard to have a Christlike
personality. But never despair in this regard, for it is possible with God's help.

[20] Among your spiritual goals should be that of imitating Jesus' joyful example more closely. (Hebrews 12:1-3)
He loved the ministry. If you are privileged to share in
the Kingdom-preaching activity, then, do not let it become mere routine. Seek to find satisfaction in teaching
others about God's Kingdom as Jesus did. Put to use the
instruction that the congregation provides to help you
improve as a teacher. And be assured that Jehovah can
give you the strength to carry out your ministry.—1 Corinthians 9:19-23.

19. What qualities can the holy spirit help you to display?
20. In what ways can you imitate Jesus in the ministry?

²¹ A dedicated, baptized person faithfully endeavoring to follow Jesus is special to God. Jehovah examines all the billions of human hearts and knows how rare such individuals are. He considers them to be treasures, "desirable things." (Haggai 2:7) Bible prophecies show that God views such ones as marked to survive the execution of his judgment soon to come upon this wicked system of things. (Ezekiel 9:1-6; Malachi 3:16, 18) Are you "rightly disposed for everlasting life"? (Acts 13:48) Is it your earnest desire to be marked as one serving God? Dedication and baptism are part of that mark, and they are essential for survival.

²² After the global Flood, Noah and his family came out of the ark into a cleansed earth. Similarly today, "a great crowd" who apply the knowledge of God in their lives and gain Jehovah's approval have the prospect of surviving the end of this wicked system of things and enjoying everlasting life on a permanently cleansed earth. (Revelation 7:9, 14) What will that life be like?

_____

21. (a) How do we know that Jehovah treasures faithful baptized individuals? (b) What shows that baptism is important to our survival of the execution of God's judgment upon this wicked system of things?
22. To what prospects may the "great crowd" look forward?

TEST YOUR KNOWLEDGE

How does Jehovah want you to use
your knowledge of him?

•

What are some steps that lead to baptism?

•

Why is baptism not an end but a beginning?

•

How can we live up to
our dedication and baptism?

CHAPTER 19

WHEN THE KNOWLEDGE OF GOD FILLS THE EARTH

SUPPOSE a great artist has just completed a splendid painting. He rightfully considers it to be very good—a masterpiece! But overnight a jealous rival defaces it. Understandably, this causes the artist great pain. How eager he is to see the vandal locked up! And you can imagine how the artist yearns to have his creation restored to its former beauty.

² Like that artist, Jehovah created a masterpiece in preparing the earth and putting mankind upon it. After creating man and woman, he pronounced all his earthly work "very good." (Genesis 1:31) Adam and Eve were God's own children, and he loved them. He envisioned a happy, glorious future for them. True, Satan led them into rebellion, but God's wonderful creation was not damaged beyond repair.—Genesis 3:23, 24; 6:11, 12.

³ God has determined to set things straight. He dearly wants to see us live the way he originally purposed. Our short and troubled existence is not "the real life," for it is far inferior to what Jehovah has in mind. "The real life" that God wants for us is "everlasting life" under perfect conditions.—1 Timothy 6:12, 19.

1, 2. How did Jehovah's creation come to be damaged?
3. What is "the real life"?

⁴ The knowledge of God brings responsibility before Jehovah. (James 4:17) But think of the blessings you will enjoy if you apply that knowledge and reach out for everlasting life. In his Word, the Bible, Jehovah God has painted a beautiful picture of what that life will be like in the Paradise earth so near at hand. Of course, as Jehovah's people we do not serve God solely out of a desire for a reward. We serve God because we love him. (Mark 12:29, 30) Moreover, we do not *earn* life by serving Jehovah. Everlasting life is a gift of God. (Romans 6:23) It will do us good to meditate on such a life because the Paradise hope reminds us of the kind of God Jehovah is —the loving "rewarder of those earnestly seeking him." (Hebrews 11:6) A hope that burns brightly in our minds and hearts will enable us to endure hardships in Satan's world.—Jeremiah 23:20.

⁵ Let us now focus our attention on the Bible-based hope of everlasting life in the future earthly Paradise. What will life be like when the knowledge of God fills the earth?

AFTER ARMAGEDDON—A PARADISE EARTH

⁶ As shown earlier, Jehovah God will soon destroy the present wicked system of things. The world is rapidly approaching what the Bible calls Har–Magedon, or Armageddon. That word may make some people think of a nuclear holocaust brought about by warring nations, but Armageddon is nothing of the kind. As Revelation 16:14-16 shows, Armageddon is "the war of the great day of God the Almighty." It is a war involving "the kings of the entire inhabited earth," or the nations. Jehovah God's Son, the appointed King, will soon ride forth into

4, 5. (a) How will the Paradise hope be realized? (b) Why should we think about our hope for the future?
6. What is Armageddon, and what will it mean for mankind?

battle. The outcome is absolutely sure. All who oppose
God's Kingdom and who are a part of Satan's wicked
system will be eliminated. Only those loyal to Jehovah
will survive.—Revelation 7:9, 14; 19:11-21.

⁷ Imagine that *you* have survived that cataclysm. What
would life be like on earth in God's promised new
world? (2 Peter 3:13) We need not speculate, for the
Bible tells us, and what it says is thrilling. We learn
that Satan and his demons will be put out of commis-
sion, locked away in an abyss of inactivity during the
Thousand Year Reign of Jesus Christ. No longer will
those wicked, malicious creatures be lurking behind the
scenes, fomenting trouble and trying to goad us into acts
of unfaithfulness against God. What a relief!—Revelation 20:1-3.

⁸ In time, all forms of sickness will vanish. (Isaiah 33:
24) The lame will then stand, walk, run, and dance on
sound, strong legs. After years of life in their world of
silence, the deaf will hear the joyous sounds around
them. The blind will gasp in awe as a rich world of col-
or and form takes shape before their eyes. (Isaiah 35:
5, 6) At last, they will see the faces of their loved ones!
Perhaps then their vision will blur just momentarily
with tears of joy.

⁹ Just think! No more eyeglasses, no more crutches
and canes, no more medicines, no more dental clinics
or hospitals! Never again will emotional illness and de-
pression rob people of happiness. No childhood will
be blighted by disease. The ravages of aging will be re-
versed. (Job 33:25) We will become healthier, stronger.
Each morning we will wake from a refreshing night's

---

7. Where will Satan and his demons be during the Thousand Year
Reign of Christ, and how will this benefit mankind?

8, 9. In the new world, what will happen to afflictions, illness, and
aging?

sleep with renewed energy, filled with vigor and eager for a new day of vibrant life and satisfying work.

¹⁰ There will be plenty of enjoyable work to be done by Armageddon survivors. They will transform the earth into a paradise. Any vestiges of the polluted old system will be cleared away. Parks and gardens will emerge in place of slums and ruined land. All will enjoy comfortable, pleasant housing. (Isaiah 65:21) As time passes, those paradisaic parts of the earth will grow and merge until the entire globe meets the standard of beauty set by the Creator back in the garden of Eden. How satisfying it will be to share in that work of restoration!

¹¹ All of this will be done under divine guidance so that the environment will not be harmed. Humans will be at peace with the animals. Instead of wantonly slaughtering them, man will resume responsible stewardship over the earth, taking good care of them. Visualize wolves and lambs, lions and calves, feeding together—and the domestic animals are totally safe. Even a little child will have nothing to fear from wild beasts, nor will the tranquillity of the new world be disrupted by cruel, ferocious people. (Isaiah 11:6-8) What a peaceful new world that will be!

MANKIND TRANSFORMED

¹² Isaiah 11:9 tells us why no harm will be done in all the earth. It says: "The earth will certainly be filled with the knowledge of Jehovah as the waters are covering the very sea." This pertains to people because animals cannot take in "the knowledge of Jehovah" and

---

10. What work assignment will Armageddon survivors undertake?
11. What will be mankind's future relationship with the earth's environment and animal life?
12. How is Isaiah 11:9 undergoing fulfillment today, and how will it be fulfilled in Paradise?

make changes, since they are governed by instinct. But the knowledge of our Creator *does* change people. No doubt you have already made some changes yourself as a result of applying the knowledge of God in your life. Millions have done so. Therefore, this prophecy has already begun to be fulfilled in those serving Jehovah. Yet, it also points to a time when people the world over will shed any animalistic or violent traits and become peaceable forever.

¹³ How grand it will be when the knowledge of God fills the earth! There will be an extensive educational program under the direction of the King Jesus Christ and his 144,000 corulers. New "scrolls" will then come into use. Evidently these are God's written instructions that will serve as a basis for educating earth's inhabitants. (Revelation 20:12) Mankind will learn, not war, but peace. All destructive weapons will be gone forever. (Psalm 46:9) Inhabitants of the new world will be taught to treat their fellow humans with love, respect, and dignity.

¹⁴ Mankind will become one united family. There will be no barriers to unity and brotherhood. (Psalm 133:1-3) No one's home will have to be locked to keep thieves out. Peace will reign in every heart, in every house, in every part of the earth.—Micah 4:4.

THE JOYOUS RESURRECTION

¹⁵ During that Millennium, the resurrection will take place. Those who willfully sinned against God's holy spirit, or active force, by unrepentantly acting contrary to its manifestation or leadings will not be resurrected.

13. What educational program will take place on the earth?
14. How will the world be different when mankind is one united family?
15. What two groups will be resurrected on earth?

(Matthew 23:15, 33; Hebrews 6:4-6) Of course, God will decide who sinned in that way. But two distinct groups will be resurrected—"the righteous and the unrighteous." (Acts 24:15) Since there will be proper order, it is reasonable to conclude that the first to be welcomed back to life on earth will be the righteous, those who served Jehovah loyally.—Hebrews 11:35-39.

[16] Instead of hearing news about wars, disasters, and death, Jehovah's servants will receive wonderful reports of the resurrection. It will be exciting to learn about the return of such faithful men and women as Abel, Enoch, Noah, Abraham, Sarah, Job, Moses, Rahab, Ruth, David, Elijah, Esther. What stirring historical facts they will present as they give background details of many Bible accounts! No doubt they and righteous ones who have died in more recent times will be just as eager to learn about the end of Satan's system and how Jehovah sanctified his holy name and vindicated his sovereignty.

[17] How helpful these faithful ones will be during the next phase of the resurrection, when billions of "the unrighteous" are released from the bonds of death! Most of mankind never had a chance to know Jehovah. Satan was 'blinding their minds.' (2 Corinthians 4:4) But the Devil's work will be undone. The unrighteous will come back to a beautiful and peaceful earth. They will be welcomed by a people well organized to teach them about Jehovah and his reigning Son, Jesus Christ. As billions of resurrected ones come to know and love their Creator, the knowledge of Jehovah will fill the earth in an unprecedented way.

---

16. (a) Who will be among "the righteous" resurrected on earth?
(b) Which faithful ones of ancient times do you particularly want to meet, and why?
17. What assistance will faithful ones give to others who are resurrected?

18 What joy the resurrection will bring to our hearts! Who has not suffered because of our enemy death? Indeed, who has not felt utterly shattered when some bond of love or friendship was torn apart as sickness, old age, accident, or violence claimed the life of a loved one? Imagine, then, the joy of reunions in Paradise. Mothers and fathers, sons and daughters, friends and relatives, will run into one another's arms, laughing and crying for joy.

PERFECTION AT LAST!

19 Throughout the Millennium, a wonderful miracle will be taking place. For mankind, it will be perhaps the most thrilling aspect of Christ's Thousand Year Reign. Jehovah will direct his Son to apply the benefits of the ransom sacrifice to each and every faithful and obedient man and woman. By that means, all sin will be removed and mankind will be raised to perfection.—1 John 2:2; Revelation 21:1-4.

20 Perfection! What will it mean? It will mean a return to life the way Adam and Eve enjoyed it before they sinned against Jehovah God. Physically, mentally, emotionally, morally, spiritually—in every way imaginable—perfect humans will fully meet God's standards. But will all people then be identical? Far from it! Jehovah's creations—trees, flowers, animals—all teach us that he loves variety. Perfect humans will have different personalities and talents. Each one will enjoy life as God meant it to be. Revelation 20:5 says: "The rest of the dead did not come to life until the thousand years were ended." Like the great crowd of Armageddon survivors,

---

18. How do you think that you will feel when welcoming resurrected loved ones?
19. What miracle will take place during the Millennium?
20. (a) What will it mean to be perfect? (b) When will Armageddon survivors and resurrected ones start to live in the fullest sense?

Do you hope to live in Paradise, when the knowledge of God fills the earth?

the resurrected ones will become fully alive when they reach sinless perfection.

²¹ Perfect humans will face one final test. At the end of the Millennium, Satan and his demons will be released from the abyss for a short time and will be permitted to make a final effort to turn people away from Jehovah. Some will put wrong desires above love of God, but this rebellion will be cut short. Jehovah will execute these selfish ones along with Satan and all his demons. All wrongdoers will then be gone forever. —Revelation 20:7-10.

WHAT WILL YOU DO?

²² Eternity will stretch out before those who love Jehovah God and dwell in the Paradise earth. We can hardly imagine their joy, and you too can share in this. Music, art, crafts—why, perfect mankind's achievements will surpass the finest works of the greatest masters in the old world! After all, humans will be perfect and will have limitless time before them. Imagine what you will be able to do as a perfect human. Think, too, of what you and fellow humans will learn about Jehovah's creation—from the billions of galaxies across the universe to the tiniest subatomic particles. Everything that mankind achieves will further delight the heart of our loving heavenly Father, Jehovah.—Psalm 150:1-6.

²³ Life then will not be boring. It will get more and more interesting as time goes on. You see, there is no end to the knowledge of God. (Romans 11:33) Throughout eternity, there will always be more to learn and new ho-

---

21. (a) What will occur at the end of Christ's Thousand Year Reign? (b) What will finally happen to Satan and all who side with him?
22. What do you look forward to doing in Paradise?
23. Why will life in Paradise never become boring?

rizons to explore. (Ecclesiastes 3:11) And as you continue to learn about Jehovah God, you will keep on living —not just a few years but forever!—Psalm 22:26.

²⁴ Is not a delightful future on a paradise earth worth any effort or sacrifice you make? Of course it is! Well, Jehovah has extended to you the key to that splendid future. That key is the knowledge of God. Will you use it?

²⁵ If you love Jehovah, you will find delight in doing his will. (1 John 5:3) As you pursue that course, what blessings you will experience! If you apply the knowledge of God, it can bring you a happier life even in this troubled world. And the future rewards are immense, for this is the knowledge that leads to everlasting life! Now is the favorable time for you to act. Be determined to live in harmony with the knowledge of God. Demonstrate your love for Jehovah. Honor his holy name and prove Satan a liar. In turn, Jehovah God, the Source of true wisdom and knowledge, will rejoice over you in his great and loving heart. (Jeremiah 31:3; Zephaniah 3:17) And he will love you forever!

24, 25. Why should you now live in harmony with the knowledge of God?

TEST YOUR KNOWLEDGE

What is "the real life"?
•
After Armageddon,
what will take place on earth?
•
Who will be resurrected on earth?
•
How will mankind become perfect
and finally be tested?
•
What is your hope regarding Paradise?

Would you welcome more information or a free home Bible study?

Write Watch Tower at appropriate address below.

ALASKA 99507: 2552 East 48th Ave., Anchorage. **ALBANIA:** Kutia Postare 118, Tiranë. **ARGENTINA:** C.F. Casilla de Correo 83 (Suc. 27B), 1427 Buenos Aires. **AUSTRALIA:** Box 280, Ingleburn, N.S.W. 2565. **AUSTRIA:** Postfach 67, A-1134 Vienna. **BAHAMAS:** Box N-1247, Nassau, N.P. **BARBADOS:** Fontabelle Rd., Bridgetown. **BELGIUM:** rue d'Argile-Potaardestraat 60, B-1950 Kraainem. **BELIZE:** Box 257, Belize City. **BENIN, REP. OF:** BP 06-1131, Cotonou. **BOLIVIA:** Casilla No. 1440, La Paz. **BRAZIL:** Caixa Postal 92, 18270-970 Tatuí, SP. **BULGARIA:** P.K. 353, Sofia 1000. **CAMEROON:** B.P. 889, Douala. **CANADA:** Box 4100, Halton Hills (Georgetown), Ontario L7G 4Y4. **CENTRAL AFRICAN REPUBLIC:** B.P. 662, Bangui. **CHILE:** Casilla 267, Puente Alto. **COLOMBIA:** Apartado Aéreo 85058, Bogotá 8, D.E. **COSTA RICA:** Apartado 10043, San José. **CÔTE D'IVOIRE (IVORY COAST), WEST AFRICA:** 06 B P 393, Abidjan 06. **CROATIA:** p.p. 417, 41001 Zagreb. **CURAÇAO, NETHERLANDS ANTILLES:** P.O. Box 4708, Willemstad. **CYPRUS:** P.O. Box 33, CY-2550 Dhali. **CZECH REPUBLIC:** P.O. Box 90, 198 00 Praha 9. **DENMARK:** Stenhusvej 28, DK-4300 Holbæk. **DOMINICAN REPUBLIC:** Apartado 1742, Santo Domingo. **ECUADOR:** Casilla 09-01-4512, Guayaquil. **EL SALVADOR:** Apartado Postal 401, San Salvador. **ENGLAND:** The Ridgeway, London NW7 1RN. **ETHIOPIA:** P.O. Box 5522, Addis Ababa. **FIJI:** Box 23, Suva. **FINLAND:** Postbox 68, FIN-01301 Vantaa 30. **FRANCE:** B.P. 63, F-92105 Boulogne-Billancourt Cedex. **FRENCH GUIANA:** 15 rue Chawari, Cogneau Larivot, 97351 Matoury. **GERMANY:** Niederselters, Am Steinfels, D-65618 Selters. **GHANA:** Box 760, Accra. **GREECE:** P.O. Box 112, GR-322 00 Thiva. **GUADELOUPE:** Monmain, 97180 Sainte Anne. **GUAM 96913:** 143 Jehovah St., Barrigada. **GUATEMALA:** Apartado postal 711, 01901 Guatemala. **GUYANA:** 50 Brickdam, Georgetown 16. **HAITI:** Post Box 185, Port-au-Prince. **HAWAII 96819:** 2055 Kam IV Rd., Honolulu. **HONDURAS:** Apartado 147, Tegucigalpa. **HONG KONG:** 4 Kent Road, Kowloon Tong. **HUNGARY:** Cserkut u. 13, H-1162 Budapest. **ICELAND:** P. O. Box 8496, IS-128 Reykjavík. **INDIA:** Post Bag 10, Lonavla, Pune Dis., Mah. 410 401. **IRELAND:** 29A Jamestown Road, Finglas, Dublin 11. **ISRAEL:** P.O. Box 961, 61-009 Tel Aviv. **ITALY:** Via della Bufalotta 1281, I-00138 Rome RM. **JAMAICA:** Box 180, Kingston 10. **JAPAN:** 1271 Nakashinden, Ebina City, Kanagawa Pref., 243-04. **KENYA:** Box 47788, Nairobi. **KOREA, REPUBLIC OF:** Box 33 Pyungtaek P. O., Kyunggido, 450-600. **LEEWARD ISLANDS:** Box 119, St. Johns, Antigua. **LIBERIA:** P.O. Box 10-0380, 1000 Monrovia 10. **LUXEMBOURG:** B. P. 2186, L-1021 Luxembourg, G. D. **MADAGASCAR:** B. P. 511, Antananarivo 101. **MALAYSIA:** 95 Bukit Beruang Heights, Jalan Bukit Beruang, 75450 Melaka. **MARTINIQUE:** Cours Campeche, Morne Tartenson, 97200 Fort de France. **MAURITIUS:** Box 54, Vacoas. **MEXICO:** Apartado Postal 896, 06002 Mexico, D. F. **MOZAMBIQUE:** Caixa Postal 2600, Maputo. **MYANMAR:** P.O. Box 62, Yangon. **NETHERLANDS:** Noordbargerstraat 77, NL-7812 AA Emmen. **NEW CALEDONIA:** B.P. 787, Nouméa. **NEW ZEALAND:** P.O. Box 142, Manurewa. **NICARAGUA:** Apartado 3587, Managua. **NIGERIA:** P.M.B. 1090, Benin City, Edo State. **NORWAY:** Gaupeveien 24, N-1914 Ytre Enebakk. **PAKISTAN:** 197-A Ahmad Block, New Garden Town, Lahore 54000. **PANAMA:** Apartado 6-2671, Zona 6A, El Dorado. **PAPUA NEW GUINEA:** Box 636, Boroko, NCD 111. **PARAGUAY:** Casilla de Correo 482, Asunción. **PERU:** Apartado 18-1055, Lima 18. **PHILIPPINES, REPUBLIC OF:** P. O. Box 2044, 1099 Manila. **POLAND:** Skr. Poczt. 13, PL-05-830 Nadarzyn. **PORTUGAL:** Apartado 91, P-2766 Estoril Codex. **PUERTO RICO 00970:** P.O. Box 3980, Guaynabo. **ROMANIA:** Str. Parfumului 22, RO-74121, Bucharest. **RUSSIA:** ul. Tankistov, 4, Solnechnoye, Sestroretzky Rayon, 189640 St. Petersburg. **SENEGAL:** B.P. 3107, Dakar. **SIERRA LEONE, WEST AFRICA:** P. O. Box 136, Freetown. **SLOVAKIA:** P.O. Box 17, 810 00 Bratislava 1. **SLOVENIA:** Poljanska cesta 77a, SLO-61000 Ljubljana. **SOLOMON ISLANDS:** P.O. Box 166, Honiara. **SOUTH AFRICA:** Private Bag X2067, Krugersdorp, 1740. **SPAIN:** Apartado postal 132, E-28850 Torrejón de Ardoz (Madrid). **SRI LANKA, REP. OF:** 711 Station Road, Wattala. **SURINAME:** P.O. Box 2914, Paramaribo. **SWEDEN:** Box 5, S-732 21 Arboga. **SWITZERLAND:** P.O. Box 225, CH-3602 Thun. **TAHITI:** B.P. 518, Papeete. **TAIWAN:** No. 3-12, 7 Lin, Shetze, Hsinwu, Taoyuan, 327. **THAILAND:** 69/1 Soi Phasuk, Sukhumwit Rd., Soi 2, Bangkok 10110. **TOGO:** B.P. 4460, Lome. **TRINIDAD AND TOBAGO, REP. OF:** Lower Rapsey Street & Laxmi Lane, Curepe. **UKRAINE:** P.O. Box 246, 290000 Lviv. **UNITED STATES OF AMERICA:** 25 Columbia Heights, Brooklyn, NY 11201-2483. **URUGUAY:** Francisco Bauzá 3372, 11600 Montevideo. **VENEZUELA:** Apartado 20.364, Caracas, DF 1020A. **WESTERN SAMOA:** P. O. Box 673, Apia. **YUGOSLAVIA, F.R.:** Milorada Mitrovića 4, YU-11 000 Belgrade. **ZAIRE, REP. OF:** B.P. 634, Limete, Kinshasa. **ZAMBIA:** Box 33459, Lusaka 10101. **ZIMBABWE:** 35 Fife Avenue, Harare.